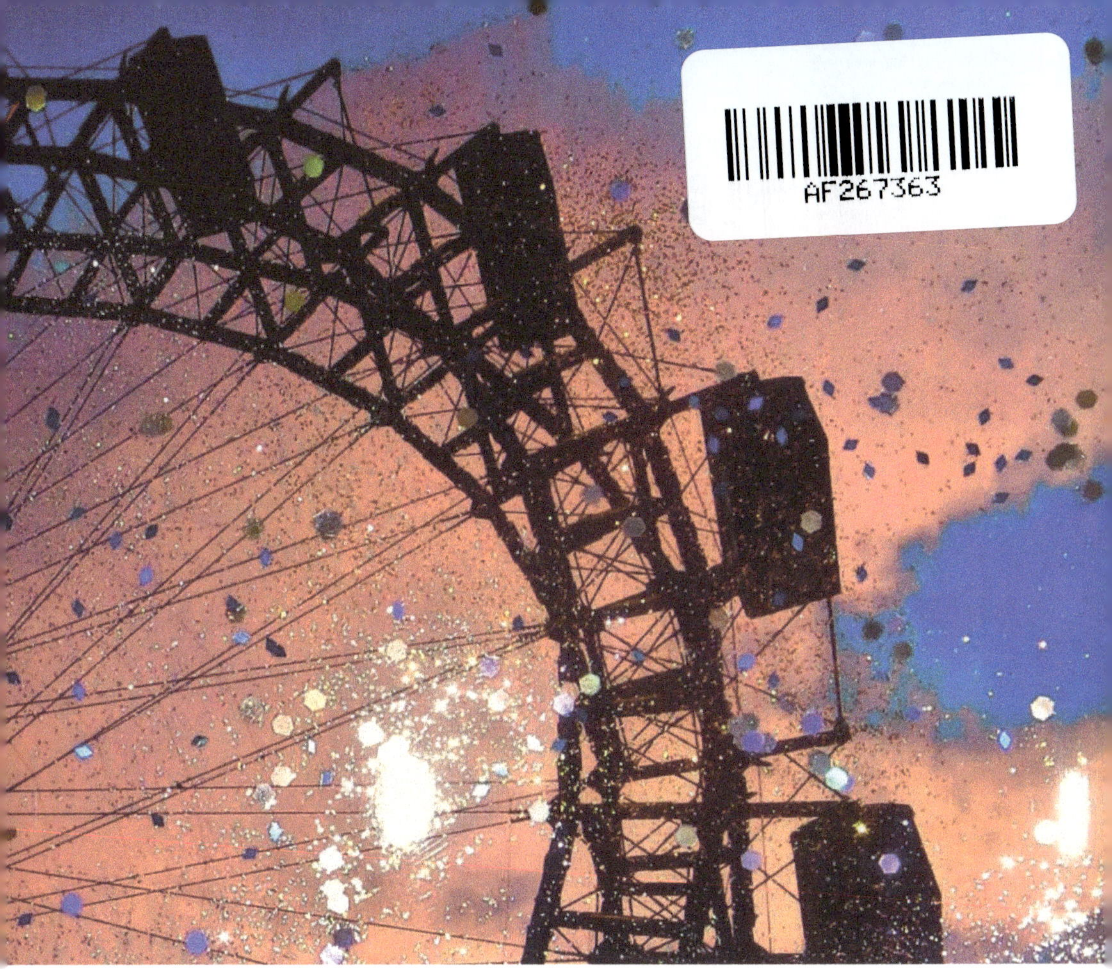

WHY HAPPINESS MAKES ME NERVOUS

Poems & Photographs
By Liza Charlesworth

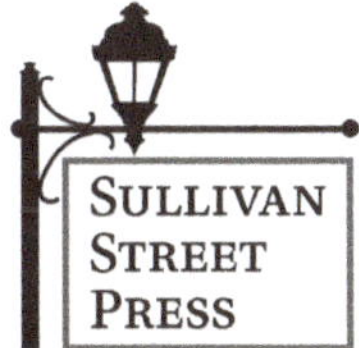

To my mother,
who taught me to look deeply
& see differently

Thanks to the editors of the following publications, where some of these poems first appeared: *Barrow Street, Bodega, Cover Magazine, Life on the Line, Mudfish, New Delta Review, Portsmouth Review, Salamander, The Boston Phoenix,* and *The Southern Review.*

Cover design by Maria Lilja
Interior design by Bethany Luckenbach

Published by Sullivan Street Press, Inc.
New York.

ISBN: 978-0-9963491-9-2

Preface

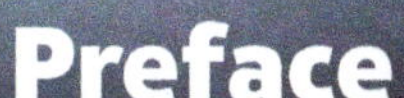

I'm in love with words and pictures. So when
Deborah Emin, the wonderful publisher of
Sullivan Street Press, invited me to create a book
that combined poetry and photography, I jumped
for proverbial joy. The project presented me with
a series of 6 x 9 canvases on which to express
myself—with the rhythm and meter of poems
and the light and shadow of photos. My goal?
To leave behind a few small stories about life on
earth in the 21st century. Welcome to my jubilant,
mournful, fractured, chromatic, curious, magical,
imperfect world! I hope you like navigating this
word-and-picture landscape as much as I liked
creating it for you.

–LC

Table of Contents

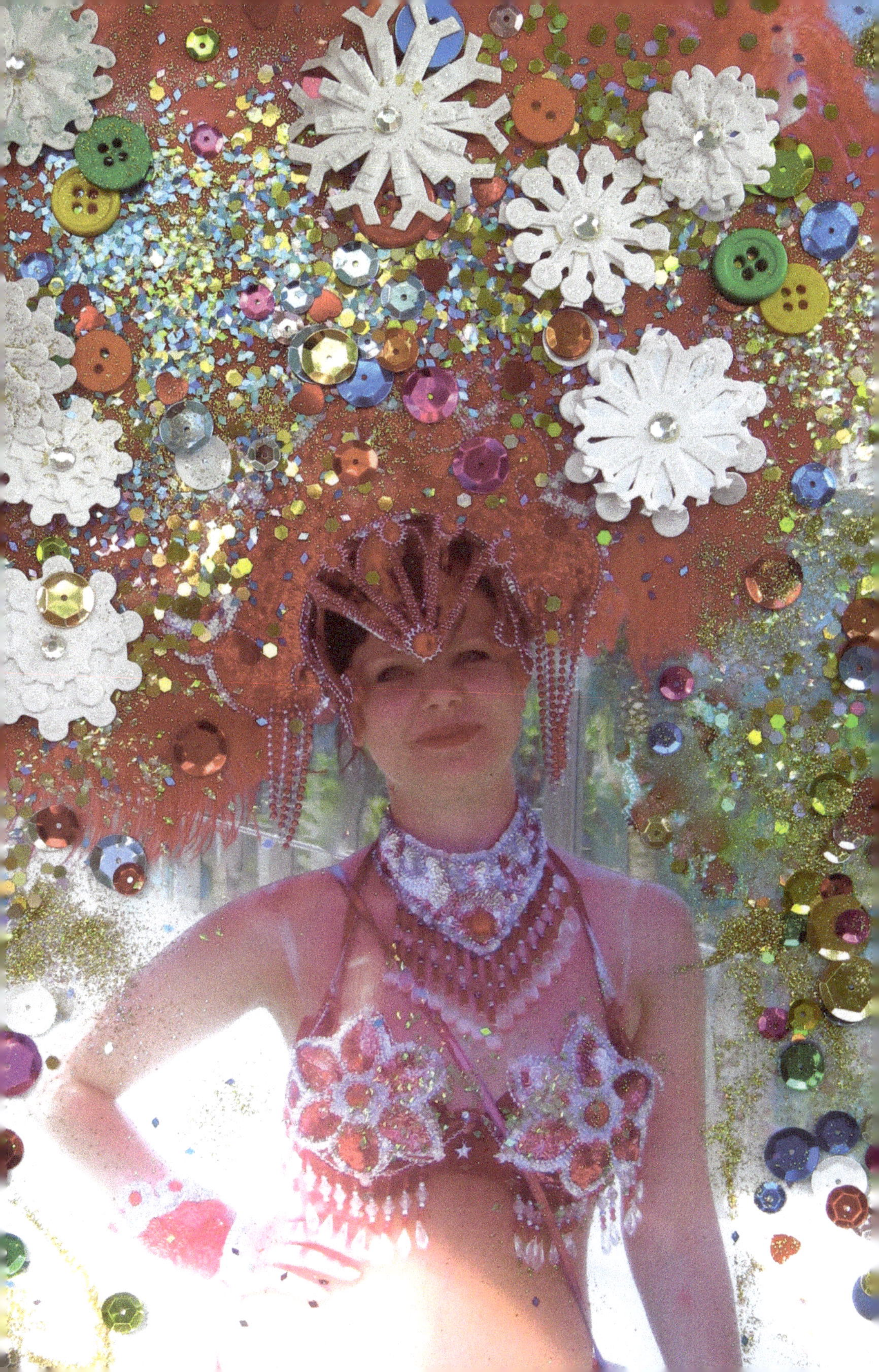

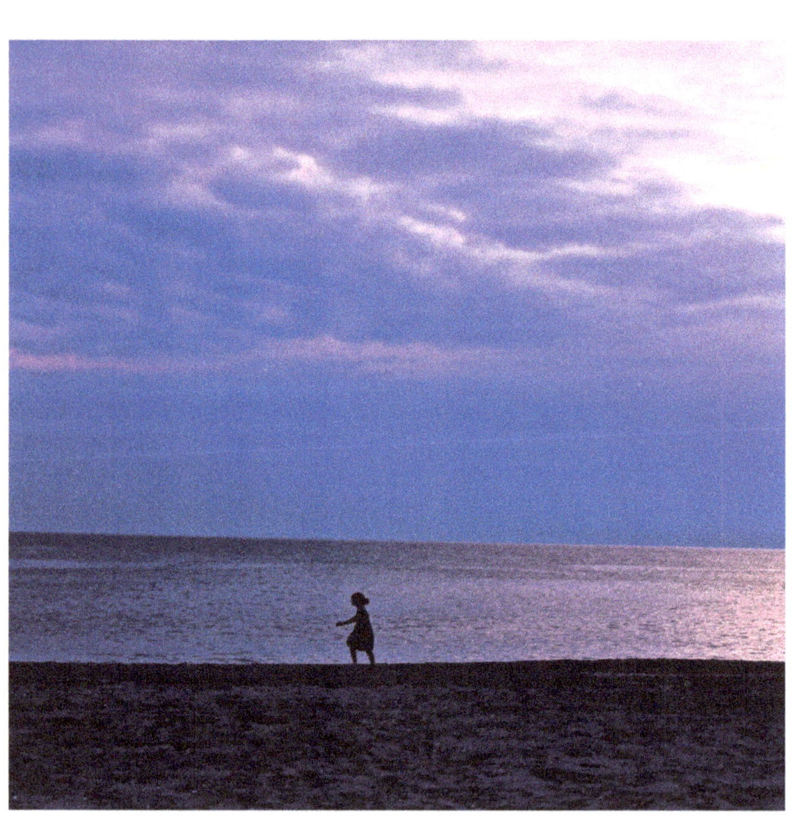

The Beauty Myth
–for Snow White

Thank the witch, for she made you a star:
her spiked apple felling you at absolute peak—
your garnet lips parted, your ripe body gone
deliciously limp. She had all the good lines,
but still couldn't compete.
Nothing trumps beauty, but beauty in peril.
After you woke, you exited to age privately
in a distant kingdom. That was wise.
That's why your fans will always see you
as you were. Not an old woman with helium chatter,
whose flesh folds behind a girdle,
whose prince rolls his eyes.

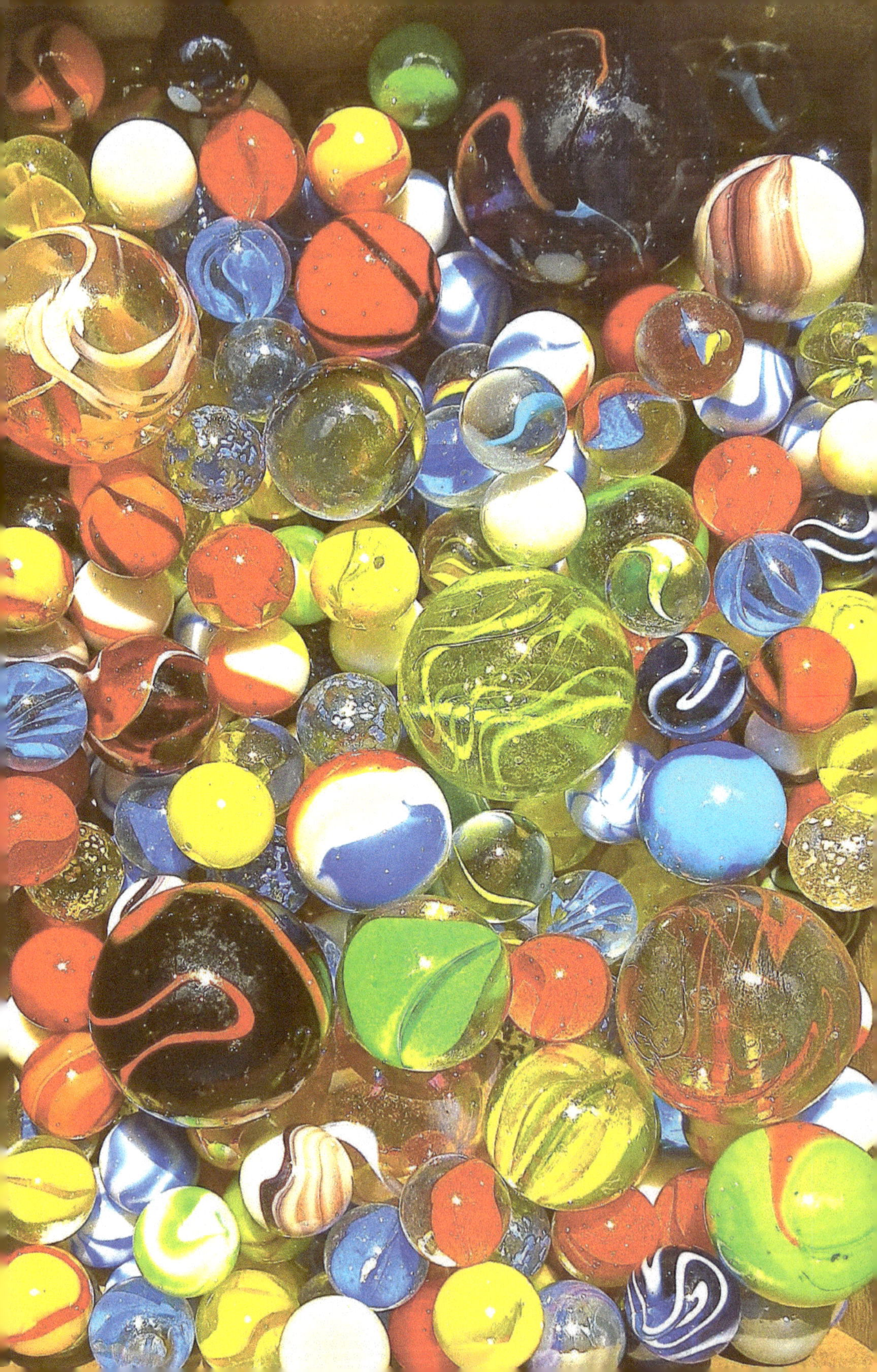

Indian Summer

Her bike's bell chirped
its warning

as she neared
then parted our epic game of four square

like a hand through hair,
sending the fall leaves

scuttling like crabs.
Kay swallowed her tune,

Pauli hugged the ball,
& all of us turned to stone

in awe of Mrs. Betty Meng,
her cancer.

I can still see her:
scarf fluttering urgently

above those peridot eyes,
her furious legs

spinning the peddles in silver circles
propelling her forward—

the plum blush of late sun
sinking

then sunken
like treasure.

The Breathing Wall

In 1976, their love flipped over
like a penny. My father's philandering,
my mother's resentment
invisibly combusting
& combusting. That entire year,
they didn't speak—silently thrusting
their plates across the kitchen table.
Night after night, the same imagined beast
drove me into their room—the metal squeak
of the box spring, my only greeting.
There, the three of us lay:
each parent locked in a private sleep,
cold as a meat locker,
with *me* breathing between them.

 WHY HAPPINESS MAKES ME NERVOUS

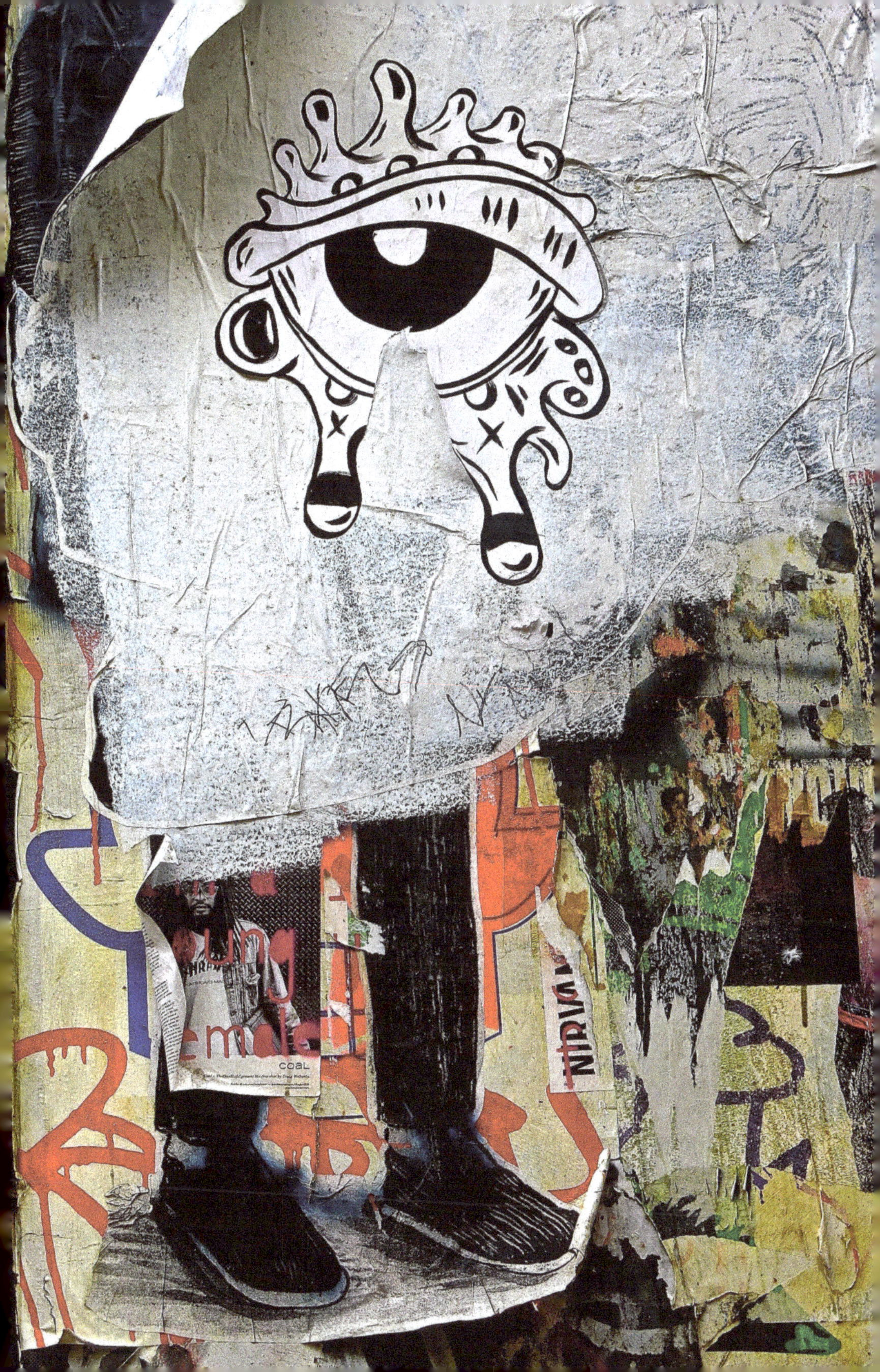

Hollywood, There They Go

I remember that day my father
came to say good-bye:
his new car idling,

his new wife,
pregnant & smiling
in the front seat

having finally won him.

He'd draw us funny pictures
& sail them through the mail, he'd call us
every night.

From the border of our straw lawn,
my sister & I waved & waved
until our palms ached;

all his bright things

pressed
against the rear window—
the cobalt road

taut
between us
& the round, remarkable sun of

California.

(There'd be babies & premieres
& a pool shaped like
a teardrop.)

As his Honda diminished—a car,
a toy car,
then nothing—

we were the ones who disappeared.

 WHY Happiness Makes Me Nervous

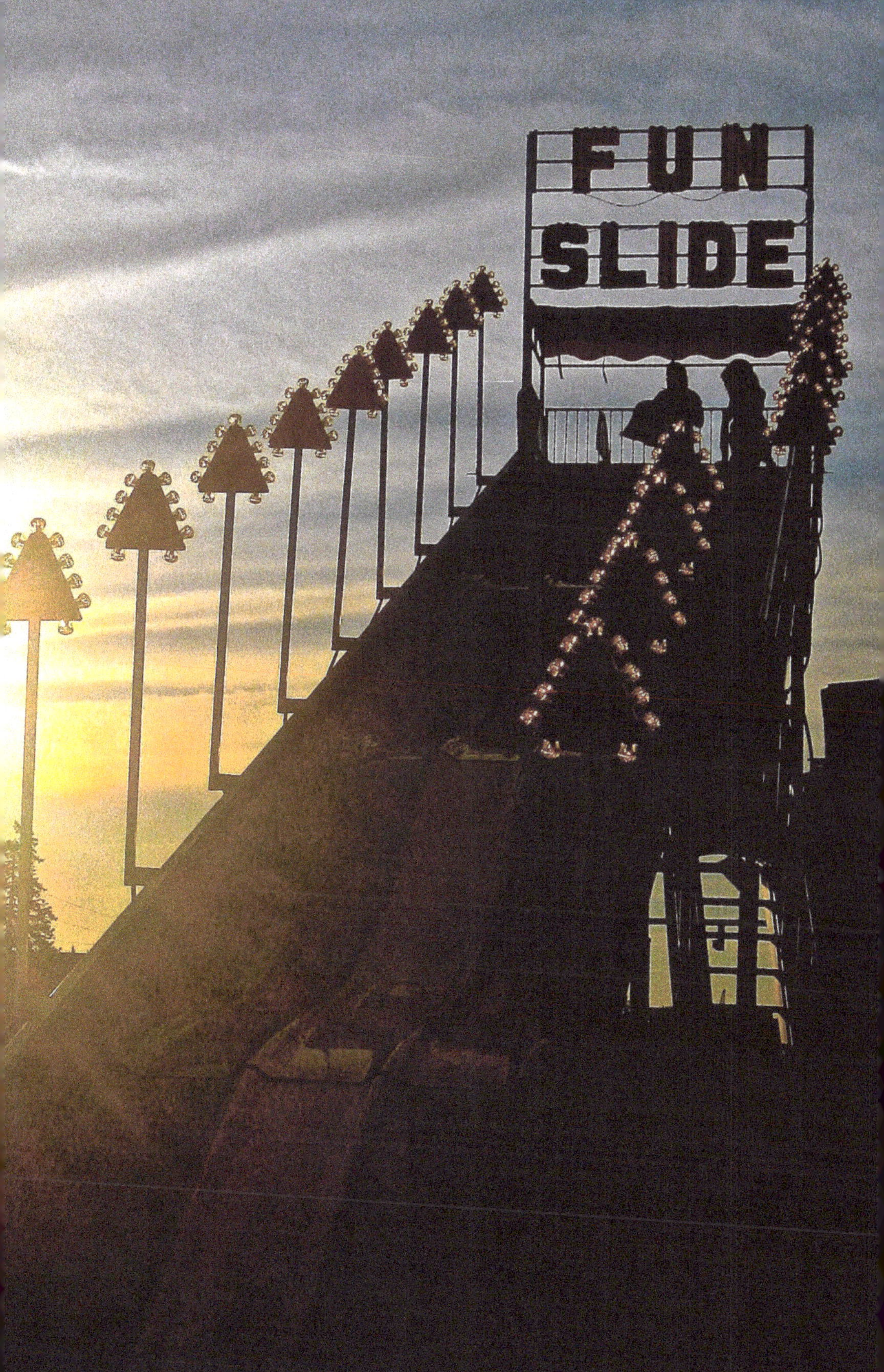
FUN
SLIDE

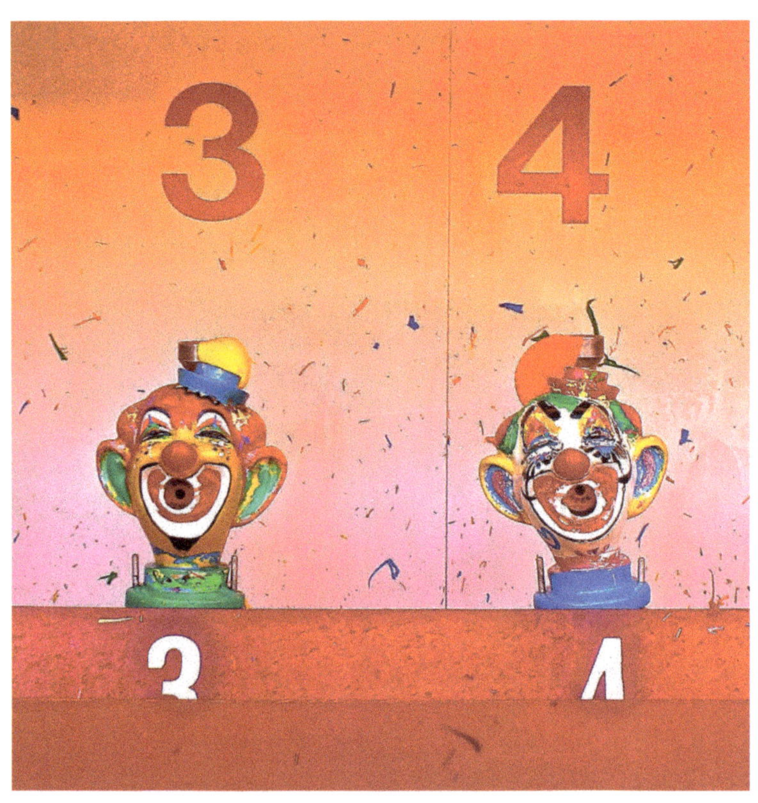

3
4
3
4

When I Was Fifteen

& every day was a desert
& every zit was a volcano
& every test was a honking scrawl of see-me-after-class red pen
& every teacher was a robot
& every father was a space alien
& every mother was a nervous breakdown
& every baby brother was a wet squeal
                        creeping across the sticky floor

& every phone call was a haven
& every cigarette was an itty-bitty suicide
& every sharp swallow of whiskey was a sip of nerve

& every boy was a pair of tramping hands & blind lips

& every car was a dark hull
      in which to fumble & lick, slur & kick,
           kiss & bite,
    hate & like.

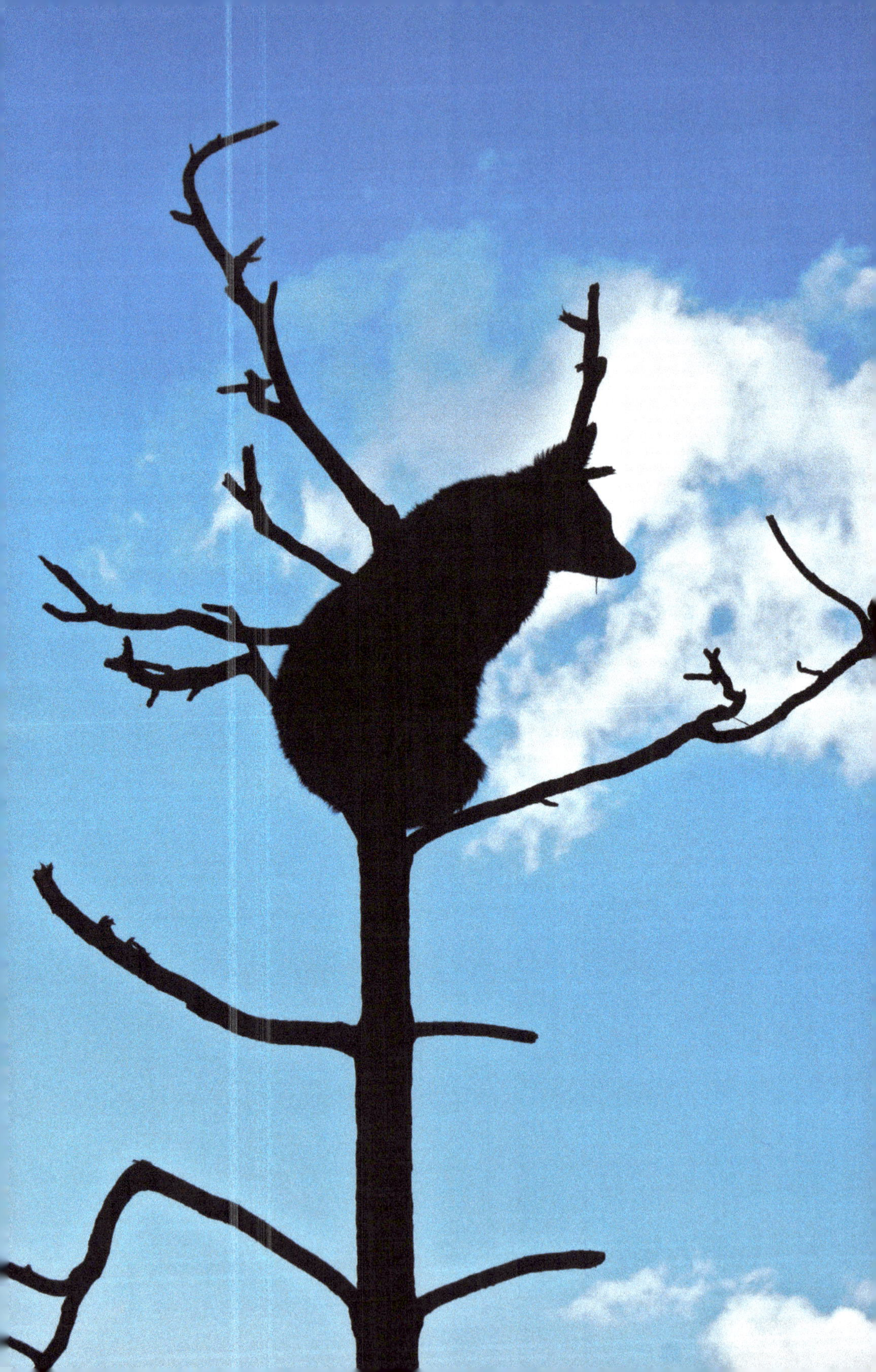

Instinct

Through a fan of fingers
I glimpse you: Quivering whiskers.
Tightrope tail. Tiny, breathing suit
of hair. Brown mouse by the radiator!
& my body screams: *Flee!*
Hurl the candlestick! Climb
the wall! But instead
I freeze. Each cell
electric—jamming my lines
with white hot telegrams
of fear. Then when I ask why,
they wire right back:
BECAUSE WE JUST DO.
BECAUSE WE JUST DO.

Love Poem From a Mirror

It's so still
I can nearly speak—a silver

whisper smooth as glass:
Hello, Hello.

& here you are
for assessment.

I need you to know
I just reflect

what I see.
For that you hate me.

But
it's *his* fault—

your split lip. Shhh.
Don't cry.

I'm longing, too:
holding

your face
just these minutes. Wait.

Don't go:
I'm the only one who loves you—

having no talent
for judgment

like the rest of them
out there.

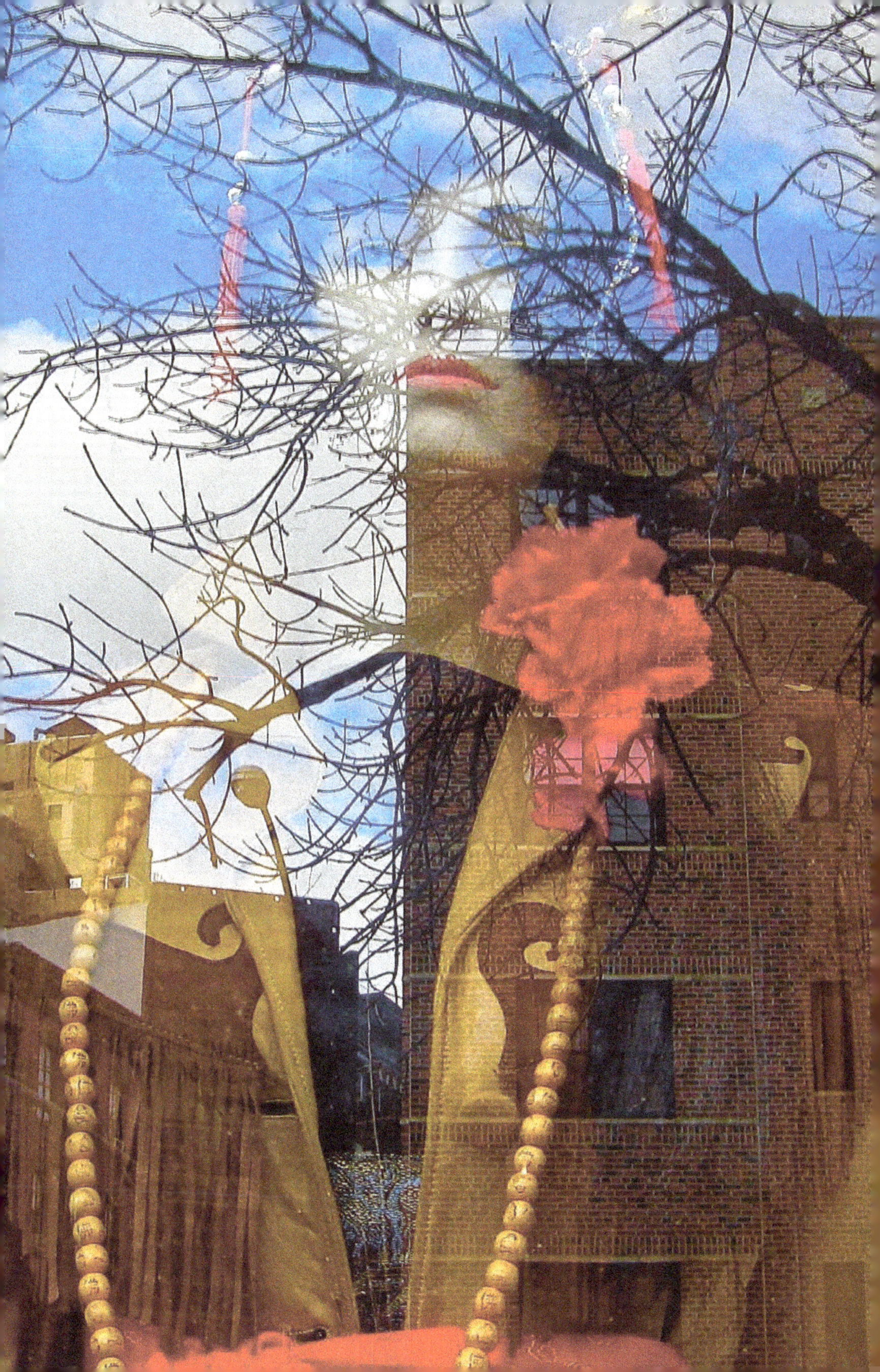

The Red Glasses

In 1978, I debuted the red glasses
in history class,
dizzied by the clarity
of Billy Moses' lips forming: "Psst!
Get a load of four-eyes' new look!"
Even my best friend, Gretchen,
withheld her support: "Why those? Why those?"

I'd made a terrible mistake!

The week before, at Meeker Optical,
I'd tried on a hundred pairs—
the "maybes" raked aside
& ceremoniously placed on a plastic tray.
Finally, it came down to two: classic wire-rim aviators
or the wild card—
big, red, round frames
"like they wear in New York!" the sales girl assured.

During the years of the red glasses,
I watched: my family rot, my dad depart,
& a patch of pimples grow
like roses
on my forehead

as girls
on the other side
glided like swans in their prestigious cliques—
whispering & expertly flirting.

"Can I *please, please* get a new pair?"
I was known to implore my father
during our weekly phone chats:
"Don't make me wait until my prescription changes . . .

I've made a terrible mistake!"

But he was resolute.
& so began a regimen
of crossing my eyes & reading in the dark
but still, the willful corneas
retained their shape.

   WHY Happiness Makes Me Nervous

At night, I dreamed heartily
in perfect 20–20
as the red glasses waited
on the night table
like a malevolent guardian angel;

sometimes, I was a cheerleader—pretty,
naked-eyed—
turning cartwheel after cartwheel . . .

content in my sleep.

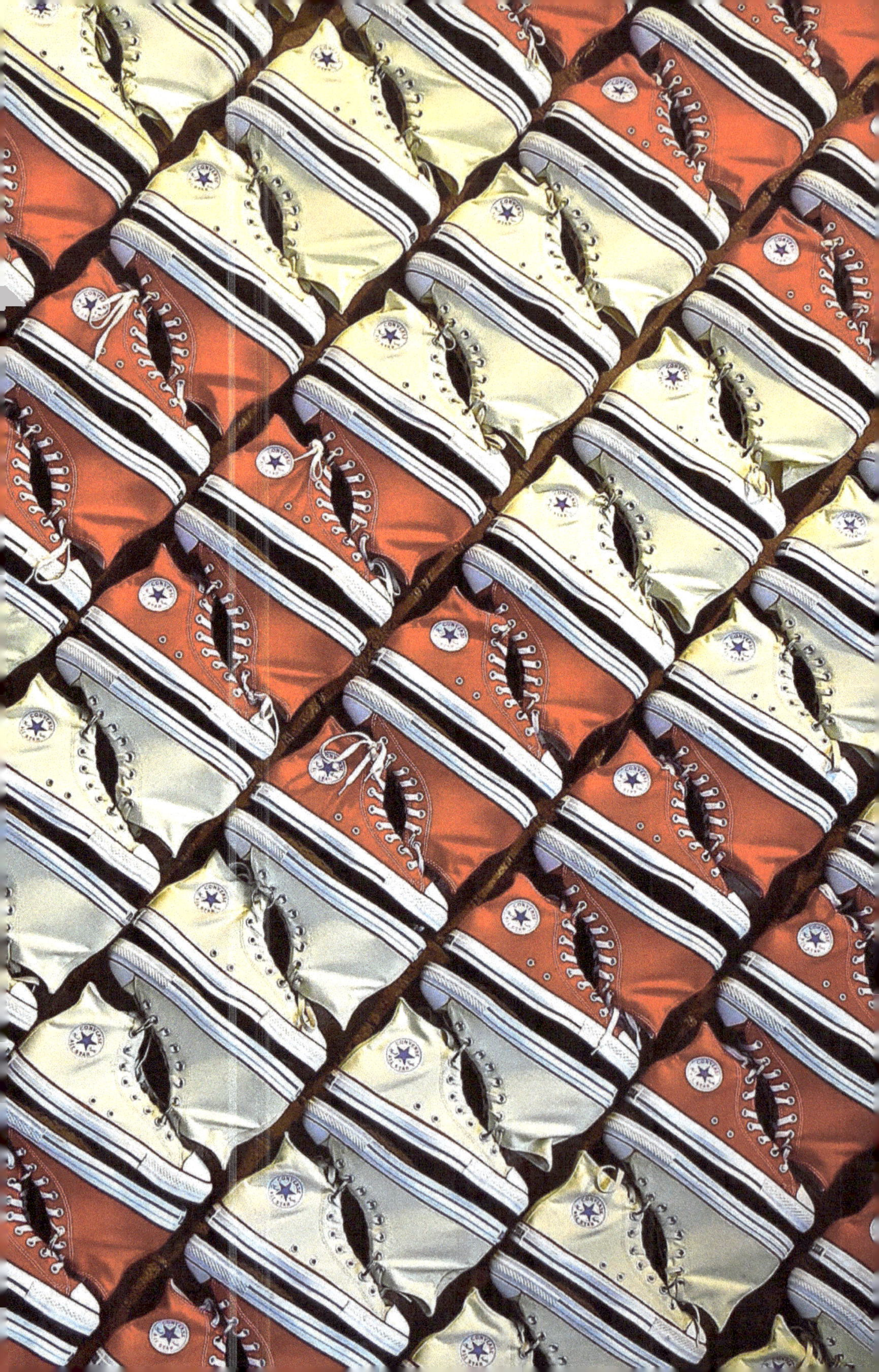

High School Story

We sat on the dock & dipped our feet into Potter Lake,
which offered up the moon & a thousand quivering stars.
The popular girls giggled & sipped beer;
I shared my Marlboros—
happy to oblige, happy the India-ink sky
helped conceal my troubled skin & unfortunate glasses.

I was out of my element you see, just treading water
among the prettiest girls in the school—
all because Katie Lister's mom
started selling Avon to mine & *insisted* that Katie be nice to me.
A bona fide miracle
I intended to take full advantage of.

As the girls traded news, I hung back & coolly nodded,
until one mentioned Margaret Krieger—
a topic I actually knew something about.
"What's the deal with weirdo & Danny Gould?" Katie asked.
& I rose to the question, like a trout to a feather-dressed lure:
"They *did it* in his Camaro, behind Tip Top Diner," I replied.

I cringe now to think of this betrayal of a friend.
But if you asked me that evening,
I'd swear that it was worth it—
my cigarette floating among theirs
like a family of fireflies,
& their regal attention as I told
                         everything.

Your Doll

Tickle my tummy.
Trim my locks with pinking shears.
Paint my eyes shut, unbutton my
frock.

I am hollow, stuffed with air.

I do not breathe.
Stick your pinkie in my mouth.
Smash
my prop-bottle &
pull down my cotton panties.

Don't be ashamed—
I have no capacity for pain.
Twist off my head,
spike it high

high into the rafters.
Stain me.

I cannot see you naked.
I will never scream.
I have no opinion of this practice.
Pull my string:
I love you
I love you . . .

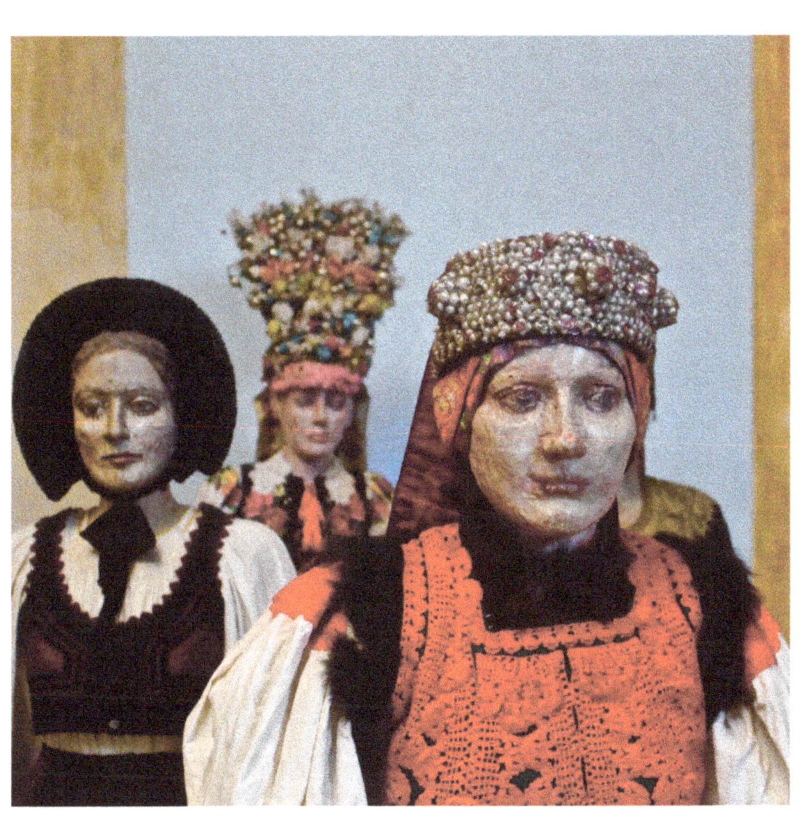

Reading in Bed With My Window Open
Onto the Airshaft

A Dominican lady singing gingerly to plants,
                    the seltzer gurgle of a baby,
        dishes stacked & a toilet flushed,
the pinched serial debate of two roommate Tolstoy scholars,
            piano chords, cat's meow,
father-son tête-à-tête,
                homerun (Mets!)
            & the bass groans of a teenage couple fucking
        all mix
            disembodied—
some doing the waltz, others the frug
menaced
            now
by a staccato scream
(female)—
barbs dropping like knives:
"You idiot! You fool!"

Then
a lush shower of tears—
        beautiful
                as diamonds.

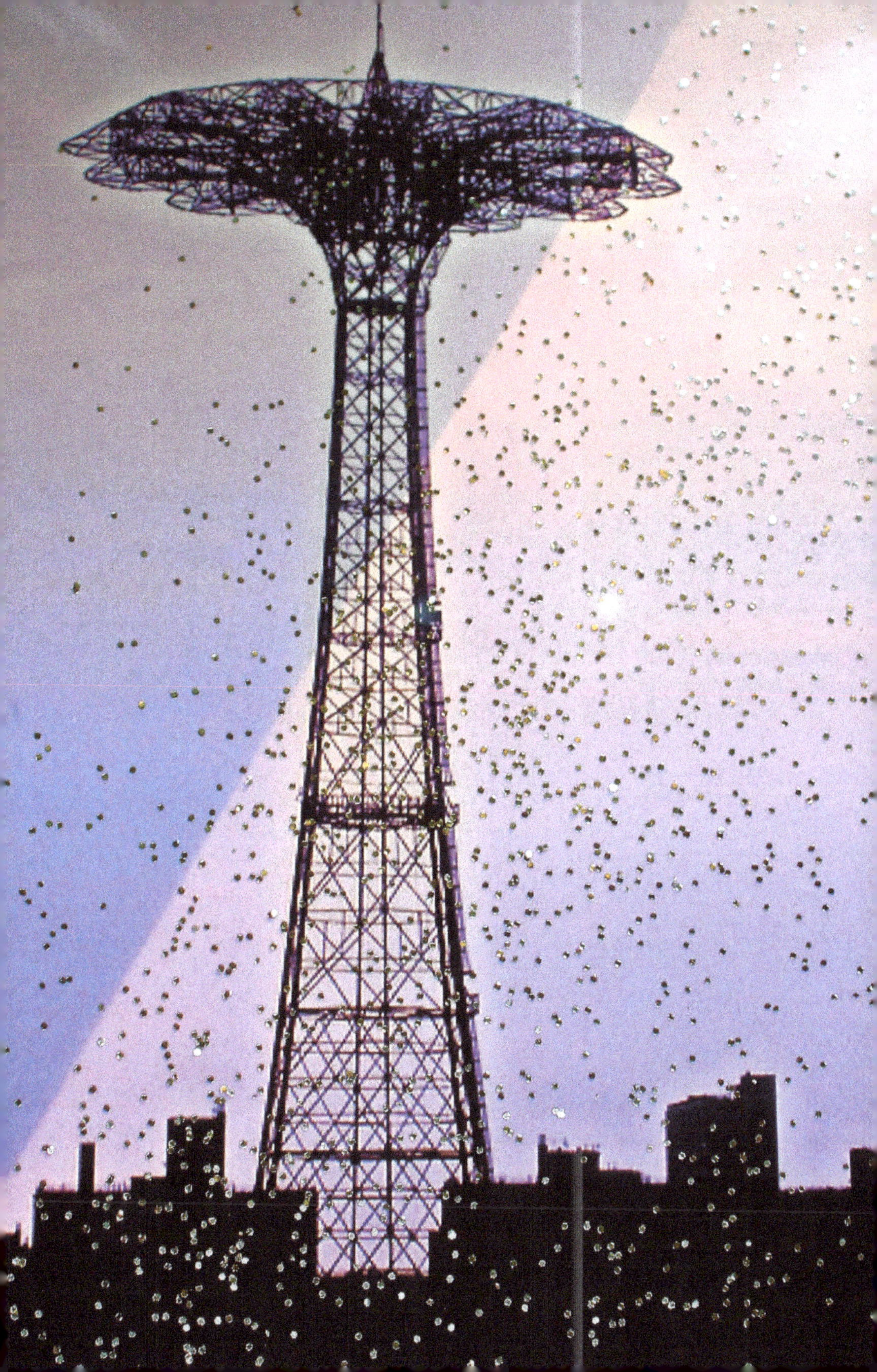

Why Happiness Makes Me Nervous

"Things are great," I tell my mother,
but somehow, this phrase stings
like a bee.
Not that it's a lie, I can honestly say
for the moment, I'm *really* happy:
loyal friends, no changing moles,
I'm an editor with two healthy ovaries in love with Manhattan
& my husband.
Yet, it's there . . .
small as a seed, black as a root cellar—
the industrial hum
of absolute terror.

Happiness is a big fat diamond
with a hairline crack, invisible to the naked eye.
Beneath the glitter of bliss
is the patient pull
of undertow. It may not get me this golden year,
but it will.
Busted loves, betrayals, fires, still births,
& terminal diseases—one for my mother & husband & me.
Don't you see?
The future holds a wall of needles
& this is the rule: We have to walk through it,
we have to.

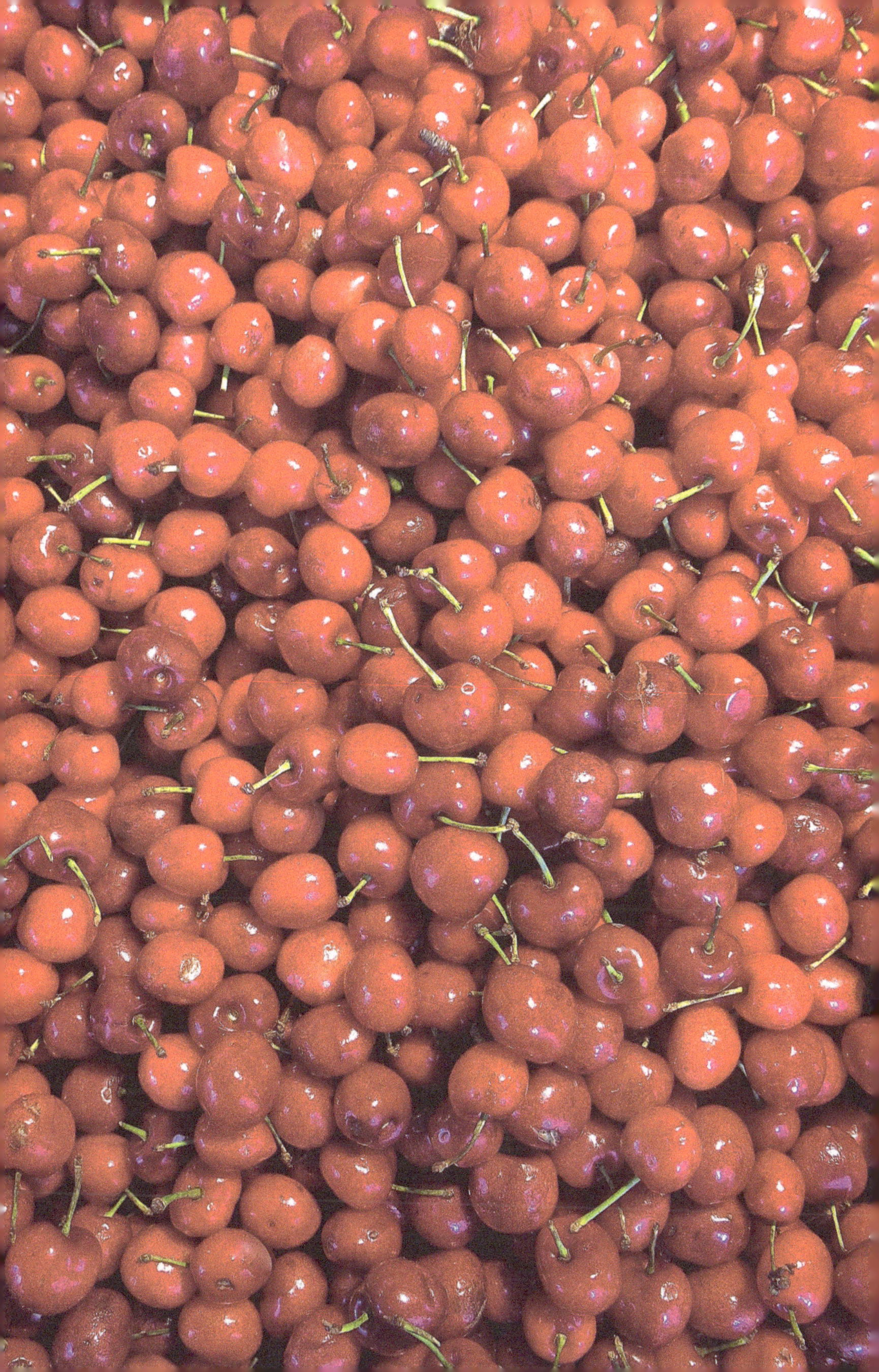

At My Grave

Kiss
our friends good-bye. Let them trickle
over the valley, back into town.
Watch their windows light
the blackening sky, glow by glow.
Know this: You don't belong there
but *here* with my lilies, my ladybugs.
Walk your fingers through
the cool letters of my epitaph.
Don't speak: Clever concepts
mean nothing tonight.
Just stretch out, over my bones,
in a canopy
of longing—good, good.
Now, stay that way.

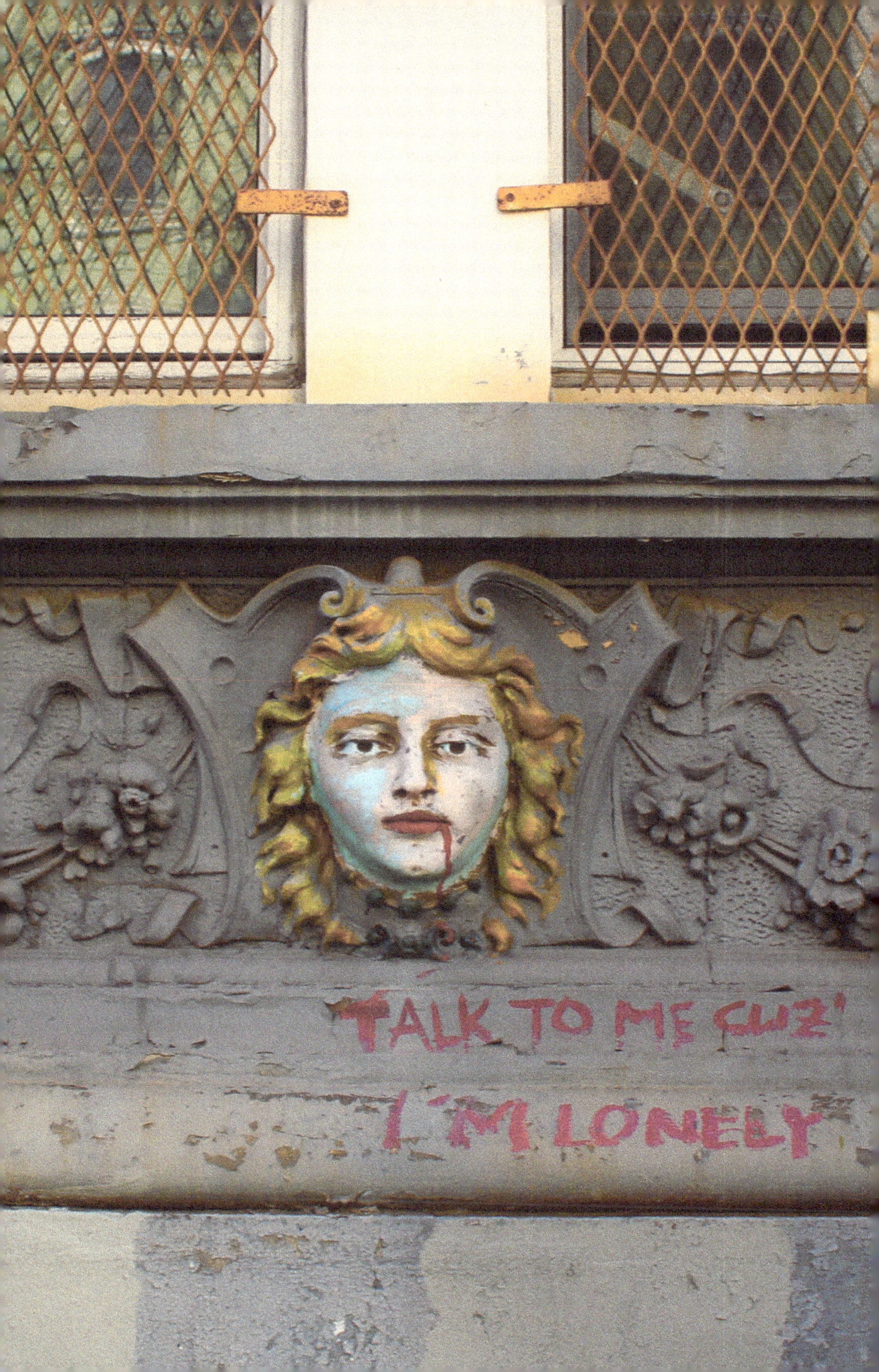
'TALK TO ME CUZ'
I'M LONELY

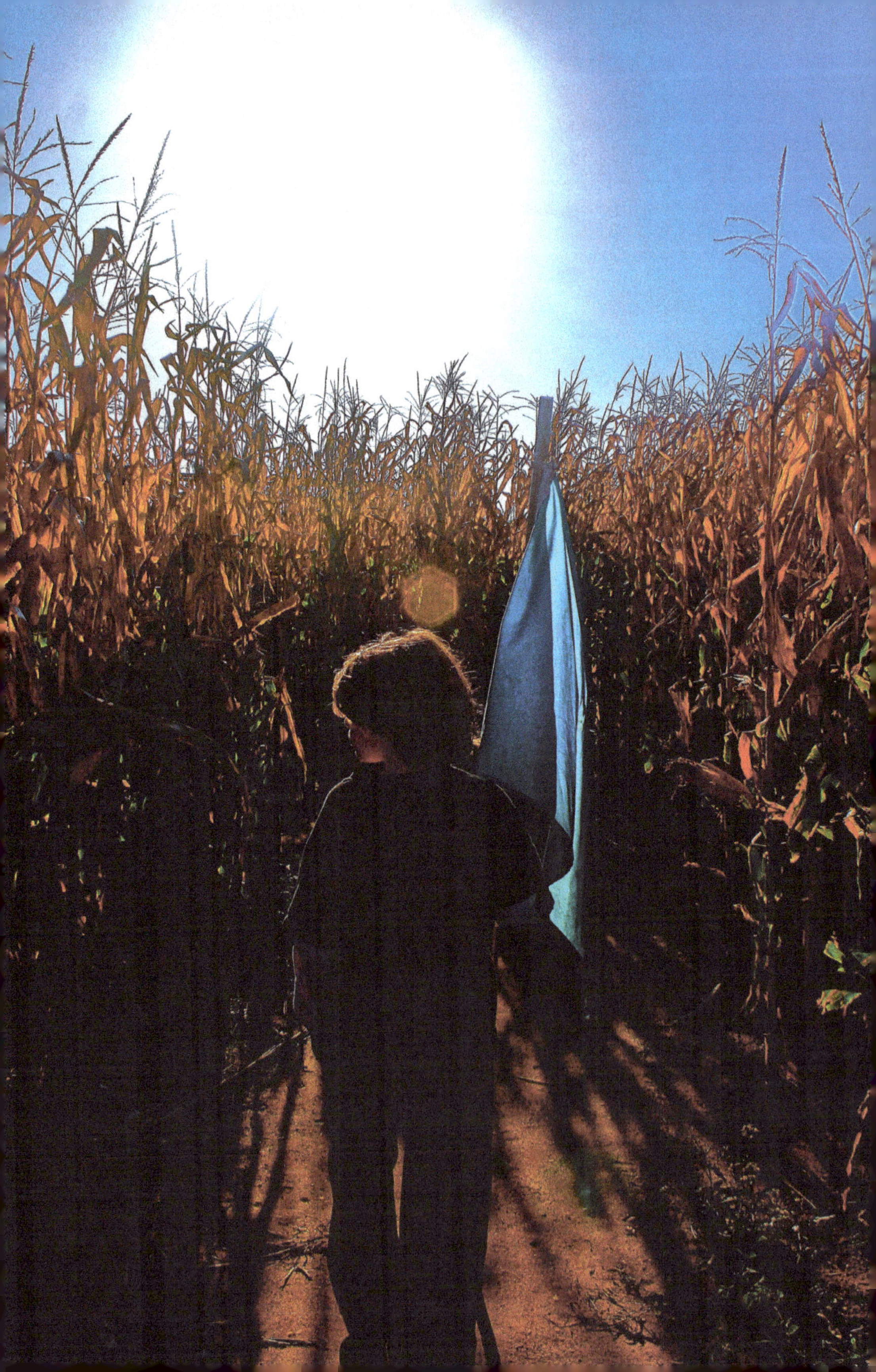

The Worrying Boy

Some children are free,
others are afflicted with responsibility—
he is such a boy.

The world is a *dangerous dangerous
dangerous* place—
a workhouse, too.

Each day there are many rituals to get through:
hands to scrub, cracks to leap,
plastic action figures to align,

doors to knock (three times),
&, most urgently,
a mountain of counting to do:

each day he must reach the summit of
four thousand one hundred & two
to be exact, no exceptions.

& if the numbers aren't said just so
(uttered too fast or too slow
or not felt precisely in his soul)

then the worry will not go.
It will rise like flood water
& bad things could happen.

This business of life is vexing & exhausting.
It makes his small heart beat
like a hummingbird.

Hours push a tedious box of yellow light
across a Star Wars rug
as the boy meticulously speaks:

*three thousand one hundred & one,
three thousand one hundred & two,
three thousand one hundred & three* . . .

as free children flash by his window on silver bikes—
their bright chirps dancing in the air like
confetti

making him lose his place:
three thousand one hundred & five?
three thousand one hundred & six?

causing all the afore-uttered numbers
to tumble like rows & rows
          of shamed dominoes . . .

Oh no! he cries to nobody.
Why did he ever agree to hold up the sky
with his ridiculous rituals?

Why is there always so much worry—
worry in his hair & pockets,
sloshing in his shoes?

He stares at a line of golden light beneath his bedroom door.
It's 6 o'clock & his mother moves to & fro on the other side,
cheerfully fussing with supper.

He wants to run out, tug on her dress—
confess that he is not, in fact, her son
       but a bone-tired-sick-secret-counting worrying boy!

Then he catches the uneasy eyes of plastic Luke Skywalker
clutching his tiny lightsaber,
     notes the blood-red sky,

feels the worry rise

& begins counting again
(to stay on the safe side):
One, two, three, four, five . . .

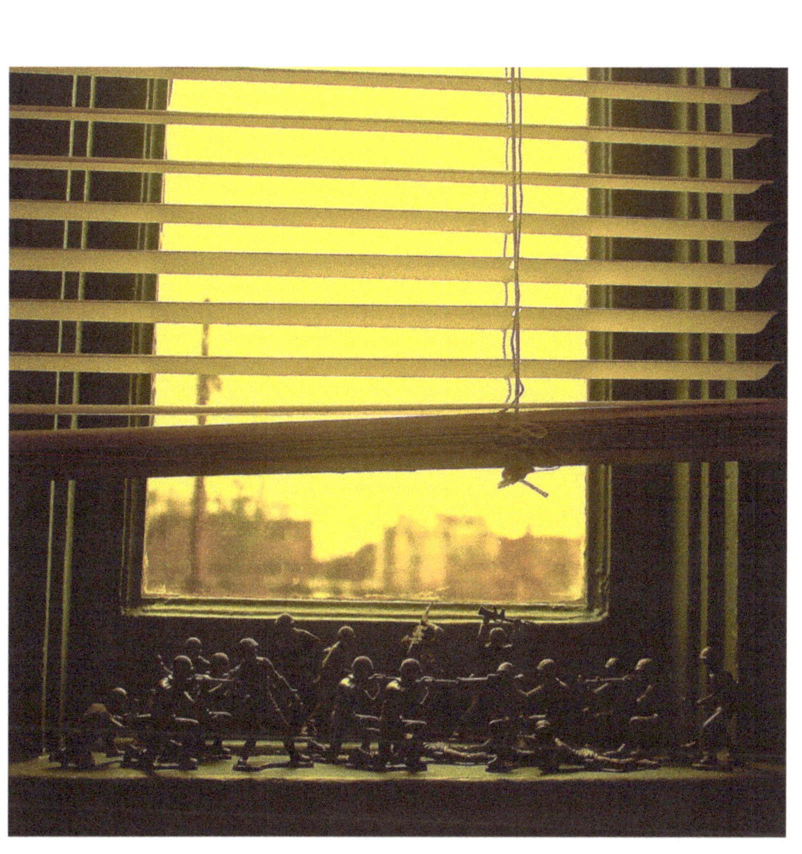

The Operation

The nurses dress you in a gown
& arrange you on a table.
The doctor positions a mask on your face
& just as you're beginning to think this gas thing
is a ruse—
  you are out

(sent to the root cellar—
no sound, no provisions,
no dreams).

While you're away, they can do what they like:
perm your hair, festoon your feet
with paper umbrellas, order an anchovy pizza
& eat it off your thigh.
But they don't, of course. They do their job:
surveying the depths of your abdomen,
equipped with microscope-probes
& state-of-the-art scalpels,

looking
  for the tiny wreck.

& when you wake, groggy as fog,
unable to locate the last seven hours
or account for your mother
rattling ice chips & smiling benevolently above,
you are surprised to find that you're still yourself
& then again, not quite—
that sour piece of you
severed,
  whisked away.

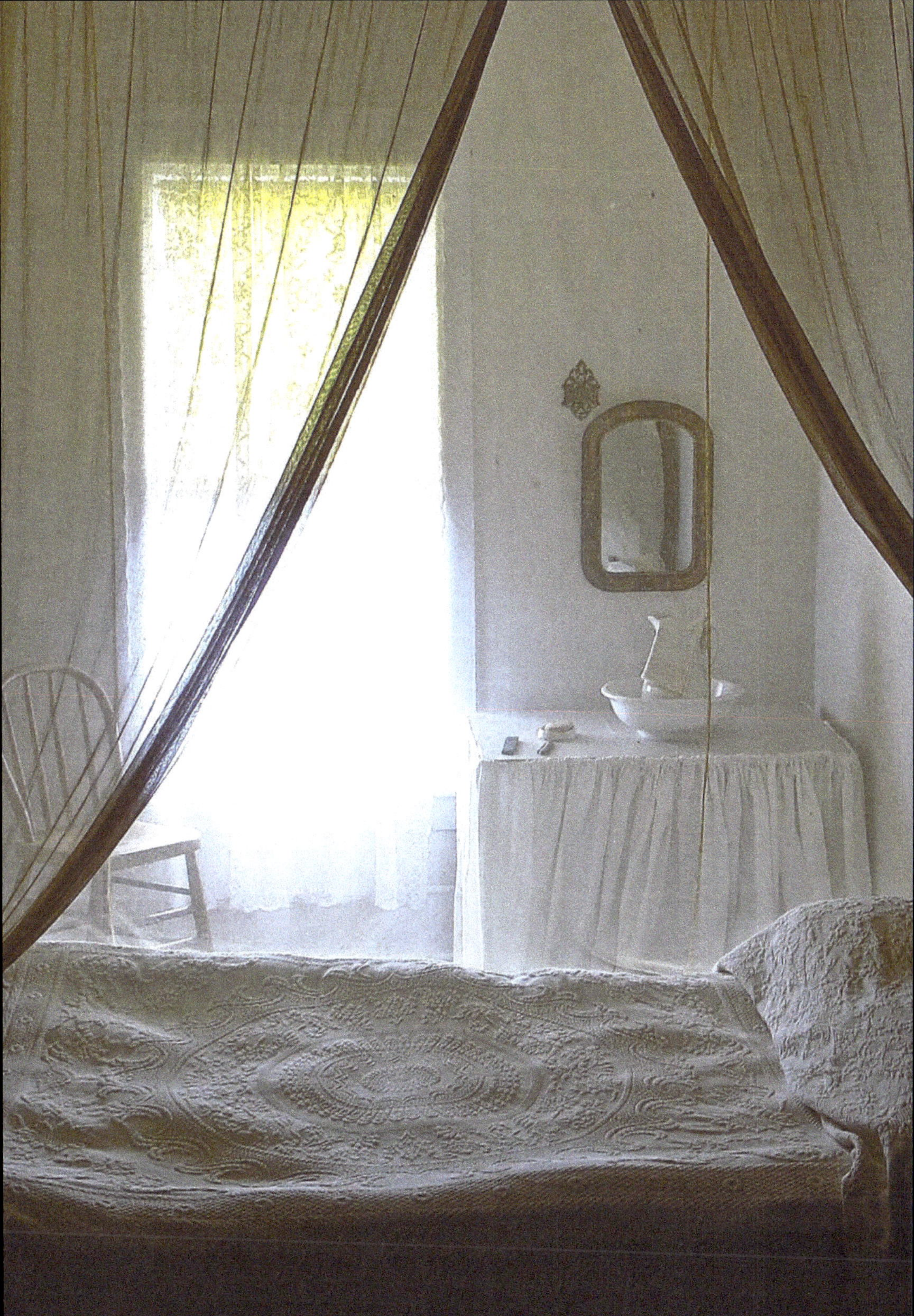

New Love

My new geography is rolling,
rolling—
unexpected, a lush atoll
for you to explore.

You ripened me.
In one stroke, I'm fearless
as a flyer
& robust as the Alps.

Your love is the most exquisite place
for which there is no name.
I unfurl
in its magnanimous glow:

arresting as a movie queen,
full
as an amphitheater.
How did you do it:

Convert my clotted poisons
to lavender,
my connotation to something epic—
the sun.

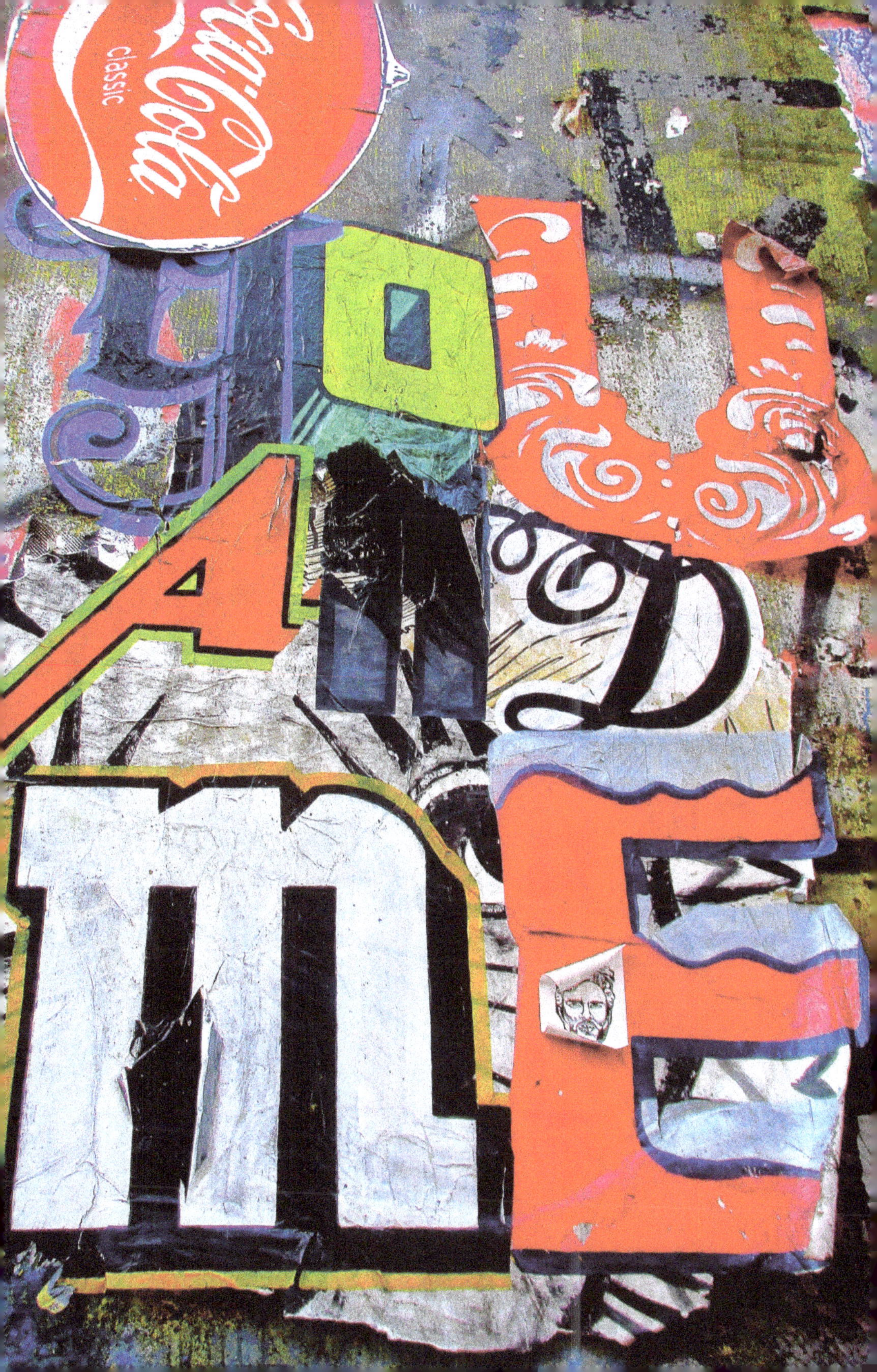

Coca-Cola
classic

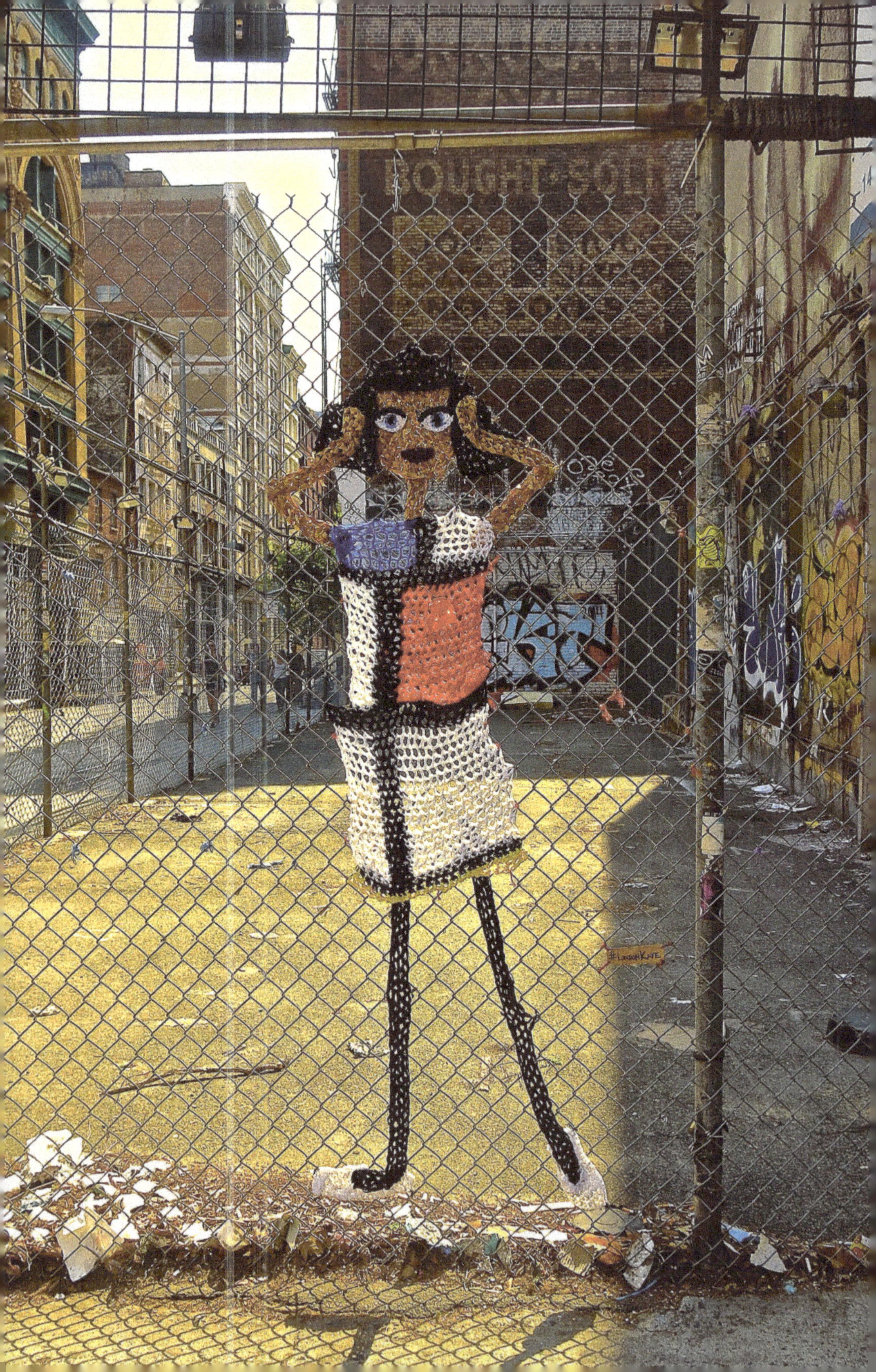

#LondonKaye

Ode to a Drag Queen

Those eyes. *Neon*. Lush lashes flutter
like hummingbirds above a sweet swell
of tits, white leather kissing your
ripe ass like milk paint. *Outrageous*.
No secret, you're so bumped on cocaine
that all your shame slipped over
God's edge. We bask in your radiant high.
How you gyrate, wrapping the music's shiny shape
around you like personal lamé. *The nerve*.
Lips dripping with frosting. We all feel
the magnetic pull of *everything*
toward your brazen bulls-eye. *Selfish*.
Sex. Object. So good, so good at it—
you make a real girl cower.
I want to be you tonight. *Bitch*.

4:36 AM

I wake like a fist
to my husband's nonsensical speaking:
"Park the corgis at the gold port"—
his breathing deep,
his eyes closed,
& I realize he's in our bed
                    & another place completely.

"They're calling me to garden top," he murmurs with a smile,
& I envision him
climbing the steep streets of Katmandu
in curled shoes red as maraschino cherries,
unfurling geishas,
or receiving a ten-tiered trophy for the best Byzantium novel
(he forgot he even wrote).

I adjust my pillow,
listening to the teeny clicks of real mice
                    crossing the varnished floor,
doubting I'll ever get back to sleep
& *my* tale involving that high-school chem test
I'm flunking in my underwear.

"Can you bring the horse butter, now?" he implores,
pausing, I imagine,
for his companion's appropriate retort
then flopping onto his side—
                    galloping true west

into that incredible dream.

    WHY HAPPINESS MAKES ME NERVOUS

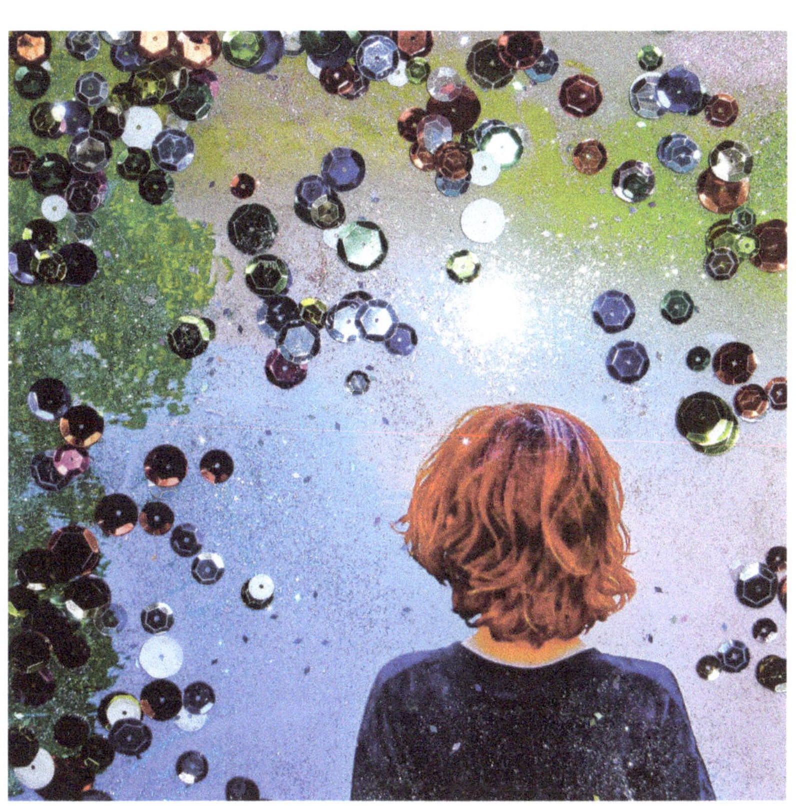

Tick Tock

Sister, it's 7:54 in the morning
and your voice comes small,
sifted through the black holes of the phone:
"I'm gonna die, I quit AA," you say,
injecting your poison
into the five minutes that remain
before I leave to get my train.
(And you know what time I get my train.)

Sister, as a king blames the messenger,
you fault Mom.
Yeah, she declared it: "Daughter you're a drunk!"
That sunny day she found you
rocked shut
from Stoli and Bombay
in a chaise lounge,
a universe away
from your fourteen-month-old son,
eating dandelions and toddling closer to the pool's
intriguing aquamarine.

Later, we sure had a good belly-laugh
at your promise to make a beeline to AA
as soon as the sun poisoning
all went away.
And you did go.
But I now know: your beginning and quitting
and beginning and quitting
is akin to the movement
of a threadless needle.

Sister, seven years ago
your disease swept me up in its twister,
depositing me in a studio apartment
2,300 miles away from you and Mom and Tucson.
Still, your machinations reach me here:
sucking the hue from all good things,
the fun from a beer, and the truth
from anyone's resolution.

　　　　　WHY HAPPINESS MAKES ME NERVOUS

I now know:
A rose is not a rose
but a drunkard's rose.
And as sure as there is rain,
I will miss this train
and possibly the next one.

I say, "Pour it all down the sink,
I think that would be the best idea,
and give Mom a call."
Now, on the crest of DTs, you plead, "Don't leave me!"

I think: *Fat chance, Sister.*
I'm Tick, Mom's Tock,
and till your liver stops,
we'll be in neat revolutions around you
like the two steady hands
of a clock.

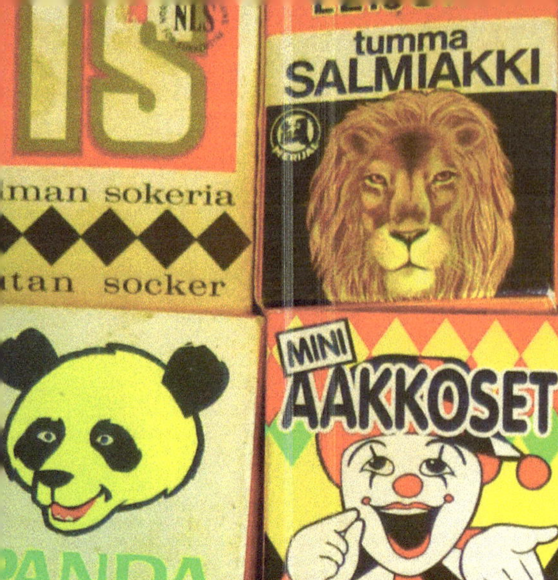
tumma
SALMIAKKI

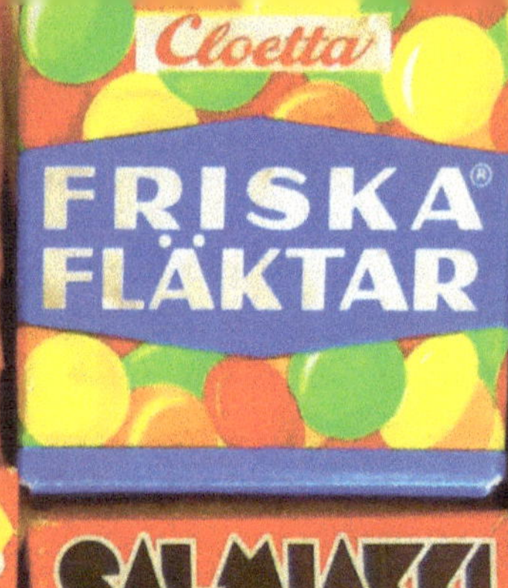
Cloetta
FRISKA
FLÄKTAR

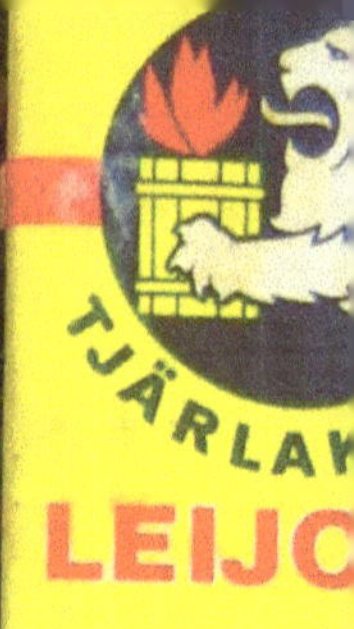
TJÄRLAK
LEIJO

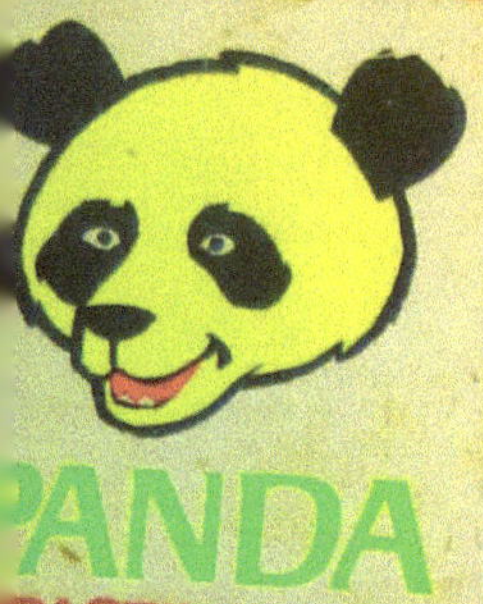
IIS
man sokeria
tan socker

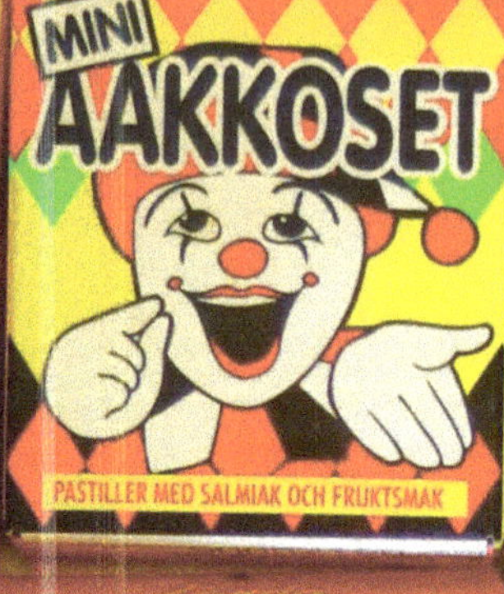
MINI
AAKKOSET
PASTILLER MED SALMIAK OCH FRUKTSMAK

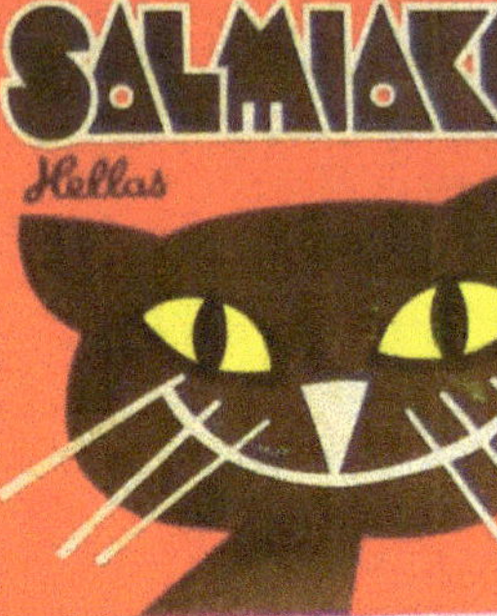
SALMIAKKI
Hellas

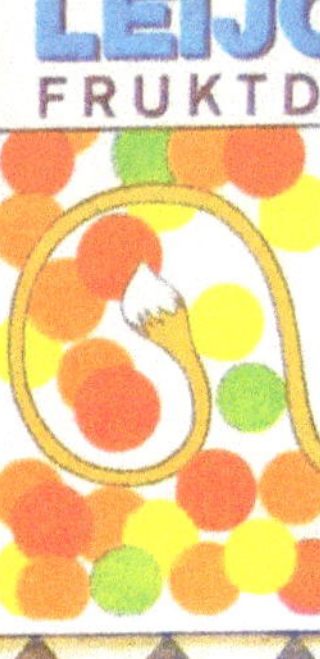
LEIJO
FRUKTD

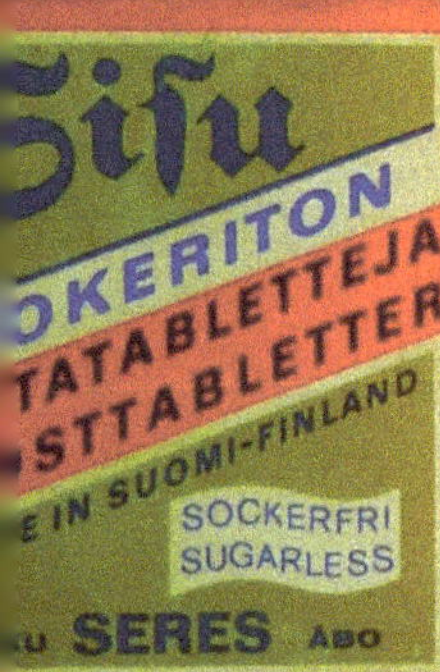
PANDA
PASTILLEJA

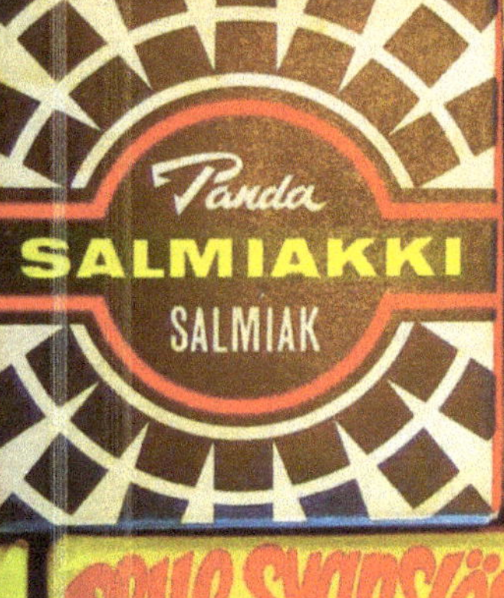
Panda
SALMIAKKI
SALMIAK

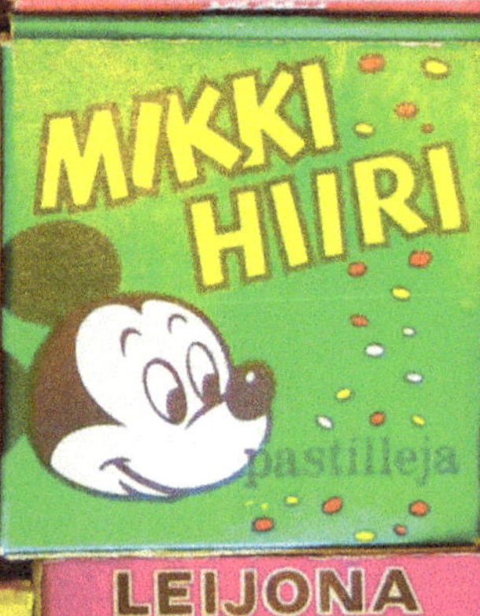
MIKKI
HIIRI
pastilleja

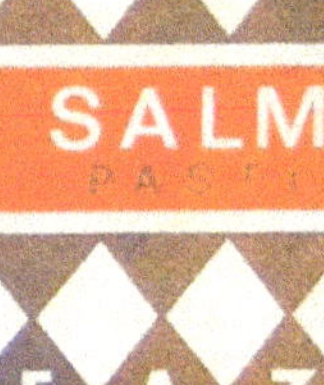
SALM
PASTI
FAZ

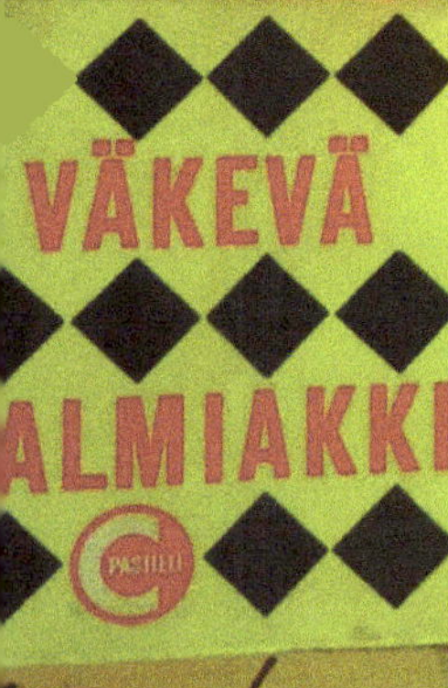
Sifu
OKERITON
TATABLETTEJA
STTABLETTER
E IN SUOMI-FINLAND
SOCKERFRI
SUGARLESS
SERES   ÅBO

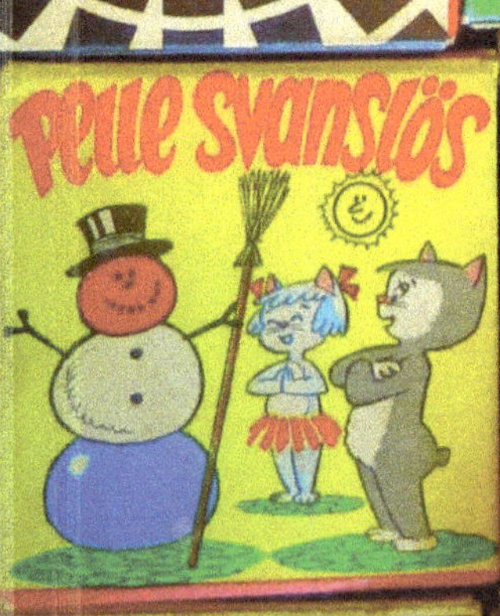
VÄKEVÄ
ALMIAKKI
PASTILLI

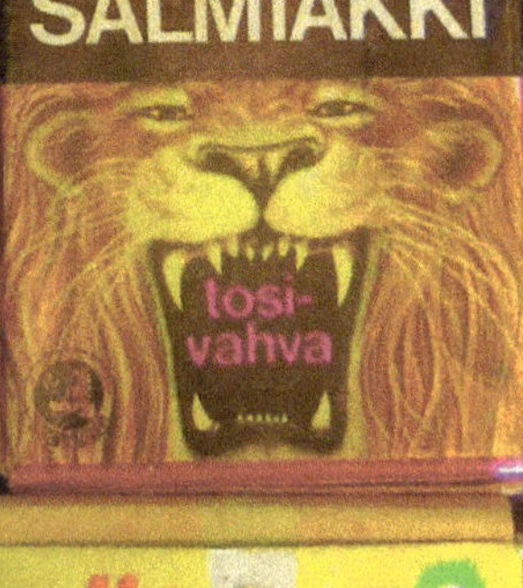
Pelle Svanslös

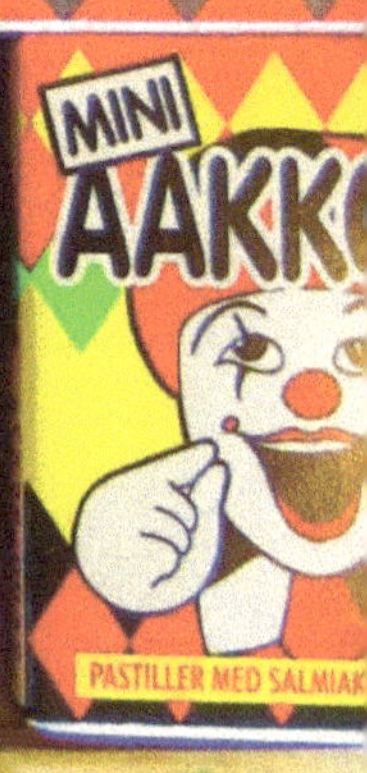
LEIJONA
SALMIAKKI
tosi-
vahva

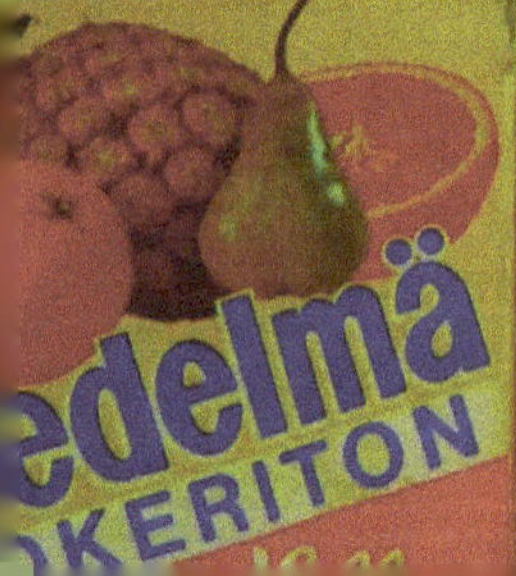
MINI
AAKK
PASTILLER MED SALMIAK

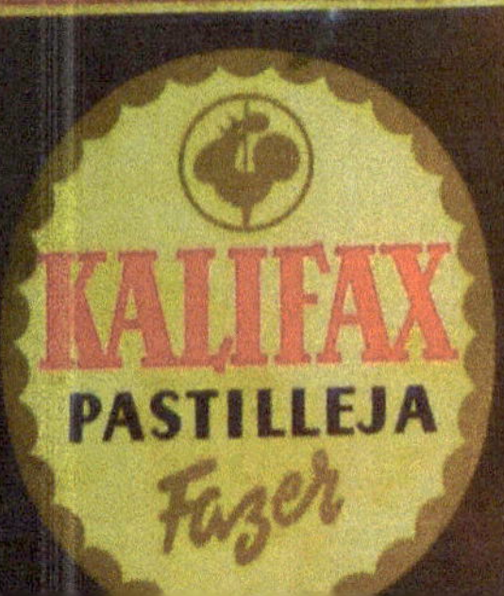
edelmä
OKERITON

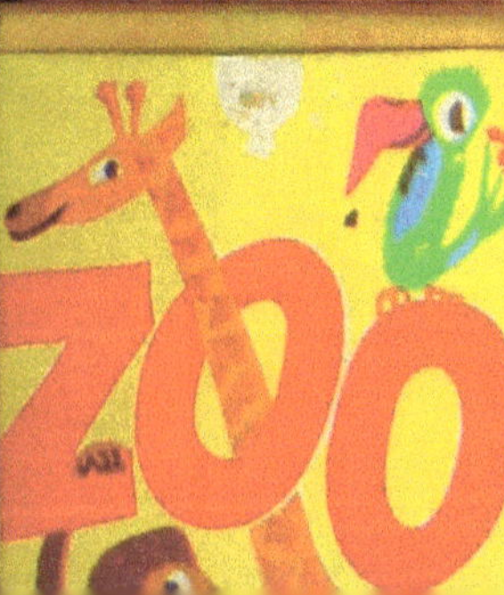
KALIFAX
PASTILLEJA
Fazer

ZOO
U.S.
Cloe
Fru

The Year You Were Joe

I love to hear about the year you were Joe
not *Julian*—
not upon moving to Olathe in '72,
a town awash in Bills and Bobs who smoked
& then tormented you.

It seems the name *Julian* was just too-too—
a heavy, fancy-pants crown on your head *everyday*
as you peddled your bike,
as you dribbled the ball,
as you monitored the ant hill in your backyard.

So, one day, you up and changed it to J-O-E—
Joe at school,
Joe at the corner store,
Joe on the sofa watching football on TV.

I hold your hand & laugh
as you tell me:

How Joe taped his hair down so it wouldn't "banana-curl"
& memorized 101 jokes to become more sociable,
& filched Camels from his Aunt Jill's purse,
& quit crying, cold turkey,
& packed away his action figures,
& declared being a cop a fitter profession than herpetology,

& simply stopped overturning every rock in the wooded lot
in pursuit of—
That yellow-bellied racer!, that blue-tailed skink!
(even though you wanted to). . . .

That's not something Joe would do.

Driving Home From Pennsylvania

Say
our Toyota
dives off this suspension bridge
under your hand's tutelage.

In that second,

will we
have a bath of
GLORIOUS
white
light
(not offered in life!)

or go
unceremoniously blank
like a TV
unplugged?

Do we meet
where freshly scrubbed souls
bob
blissfully ever after

or just become
two busted kits
of skin-bones-blood
poked at by hands in plastic gloves?

Will I shriek:
"You————-!,"
searching the envelope of that instant
for an uninvented expletive
to prick your blue eye
like an ice pick

or sing
with divine inflection: "I wasn't expecting it—
but thank you,
thank you
for this accident."

     WHY HAPPINESS MAKES ME NERVOUS

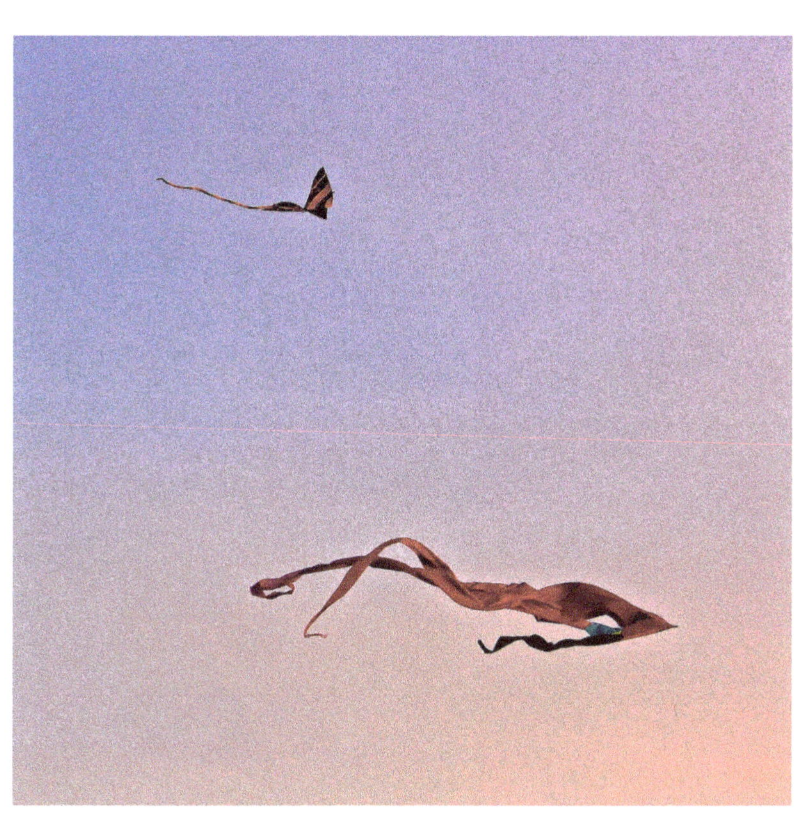

A Leaf Upon Finally Freeing Itself
From the Old Maple Tree

For years
I could drink:

Bring on the rain!
Falling

Falling.
Impossible—

This sky movie!
Here I lie

Fitfully.
Kiss me

I'm burning up!
My skin:

A paper glove
Of radiant

Red.
More compelling

I have never been.
How do you

Do?
Flirting cattails

Sticks & snails
Sweet bed

Of mud—
The exquisite underworld

I so long dreamed!
Down down

Down
Here.

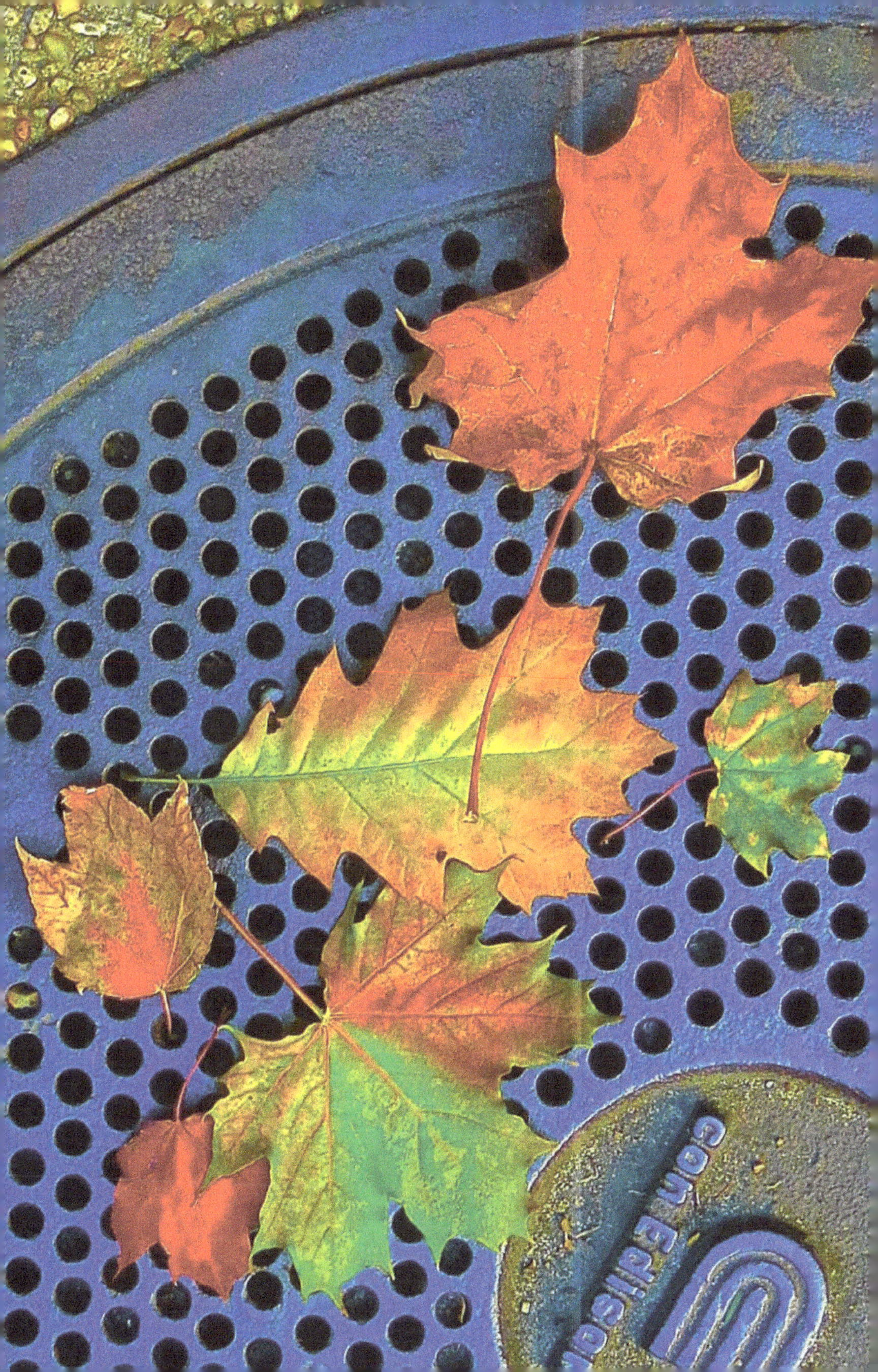

Repair
—for my friend

Penetrate the silver skin of a lake
to find its truth: chaos
of weeds, fish
eating fish.

The day
you called out of the blue
(from jail
for me to bail you out)

I saw you sob.
I saw
your perfect face shatter
& rain.

(I hadn't a clue.)

Today
on the occasion of your 376th day clean,
on the heels of a thousand
gorgeous apologies:

You tell me you love me,
& I frisk your soft voice
for the meaning
beneath.

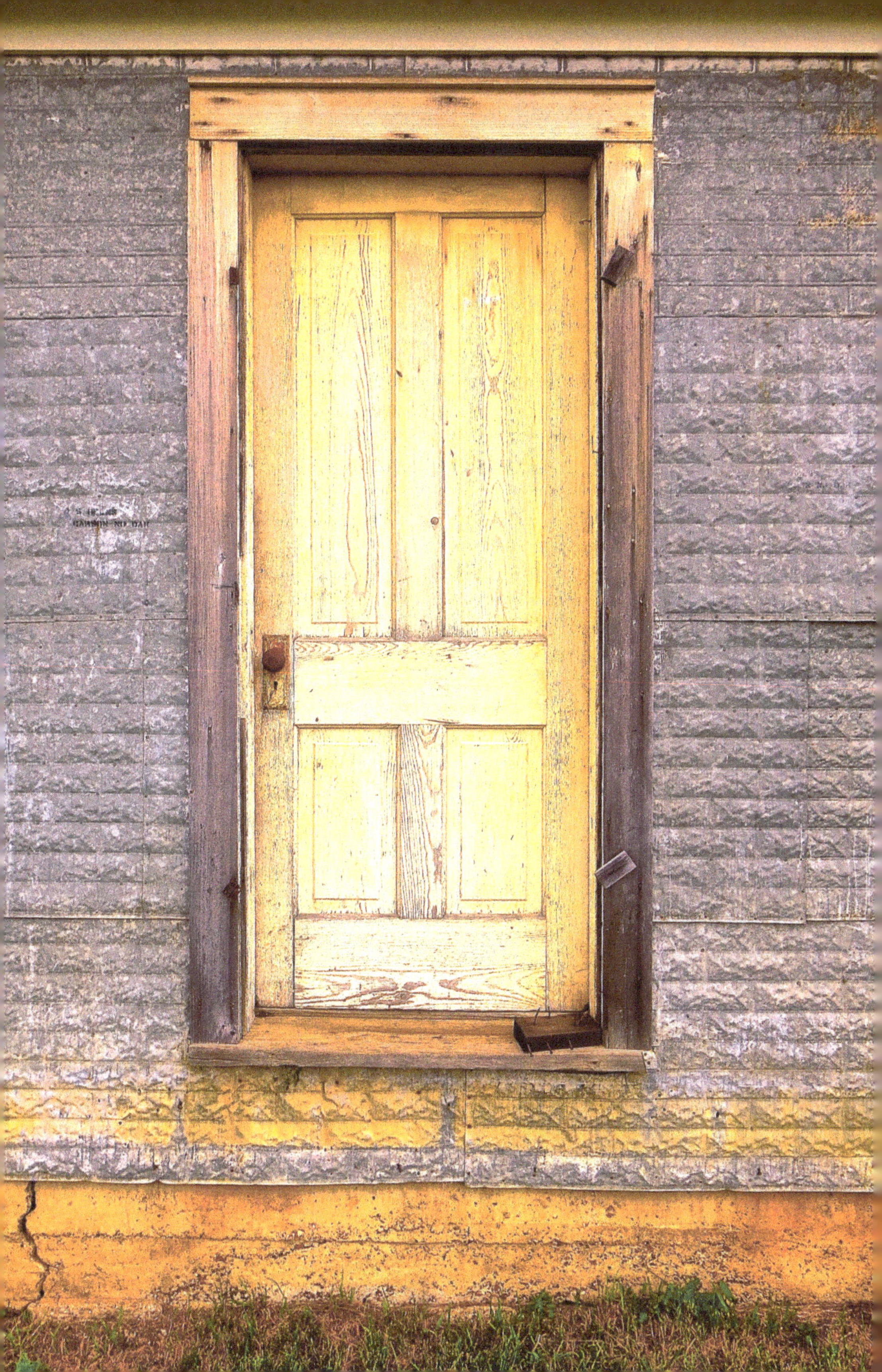

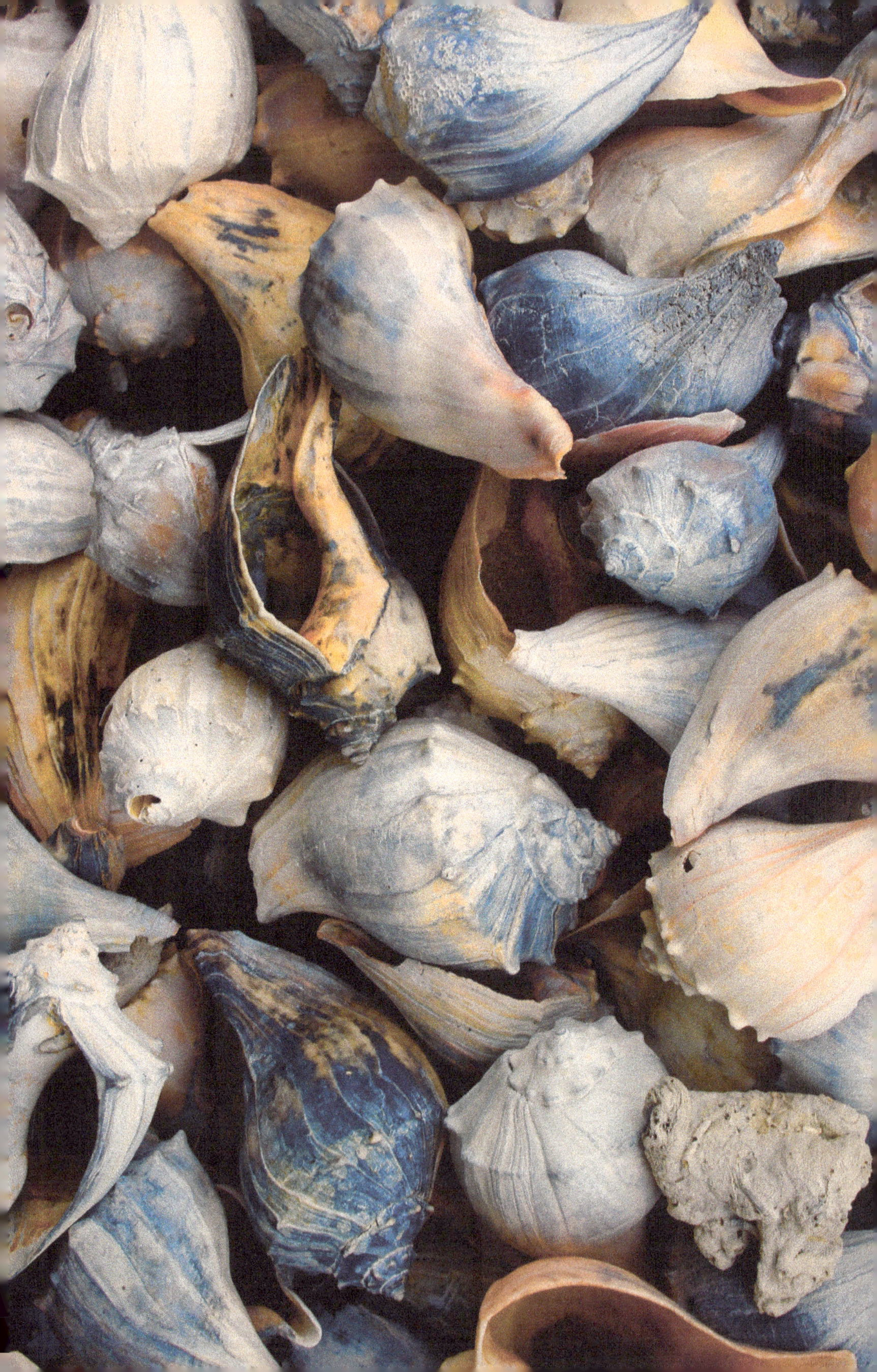

It Must Be Recorded

Write down "had a friend."
Write down "long ago."

Write down that the Atlantic looked exquisitely inviting at night.

Write down there was no alcohol consumed,
absolutely no altercation as reported—
    Never never never.
       God!

Write down that two designated chaperones
    positioned on the beach panicked.
Write down that it was ~~their fault,~~
~~our fault, his fault—~~

horseplay.

Write down that the rest of us suffered.
Mention also that we prospered: graduated high school/married/

moved away.

Fill the margins with all the scrawled details anyone can recall

then file the document
in the sand

because he is still gone
& it must be recorded.

Bliss at the Beach House

I stand at the window,
wearing your sex-scent
like a kid glove
as you sleep, artistically
tangled in the sheet. The sea rolls its rhymes.

The stars were the final requirement
& here they are:
pricking the purple-black sky
spectacularly!

All the cruelties we made
& exchanged—
skillfully licked to sharper then sharper
icicles—
are just water in that pitcher,
tonight.

In this light,
my skin is equal to white lilies.
I am not a classic beauty,
but *more* complex.
I am thirty & have no children
but I will, I will have them.

& the best friend I ever knew
& buried last winter
is not unblissful;
he's whispering to the sand: *I could get used to you.*

The ocean reminds me
that the unsettling rise & fall
of needing & receiving,
& needing & not receiving,
may return tomorrow
but I don't care—

this night is so
expansive.

Everything I need is here:
the ocean, the sky, you,
& all the words—
waiting to come up at the root

like salt grass from a dune.
I could write the perfect poem
if I tried,
but it is not required,
nothing is required.

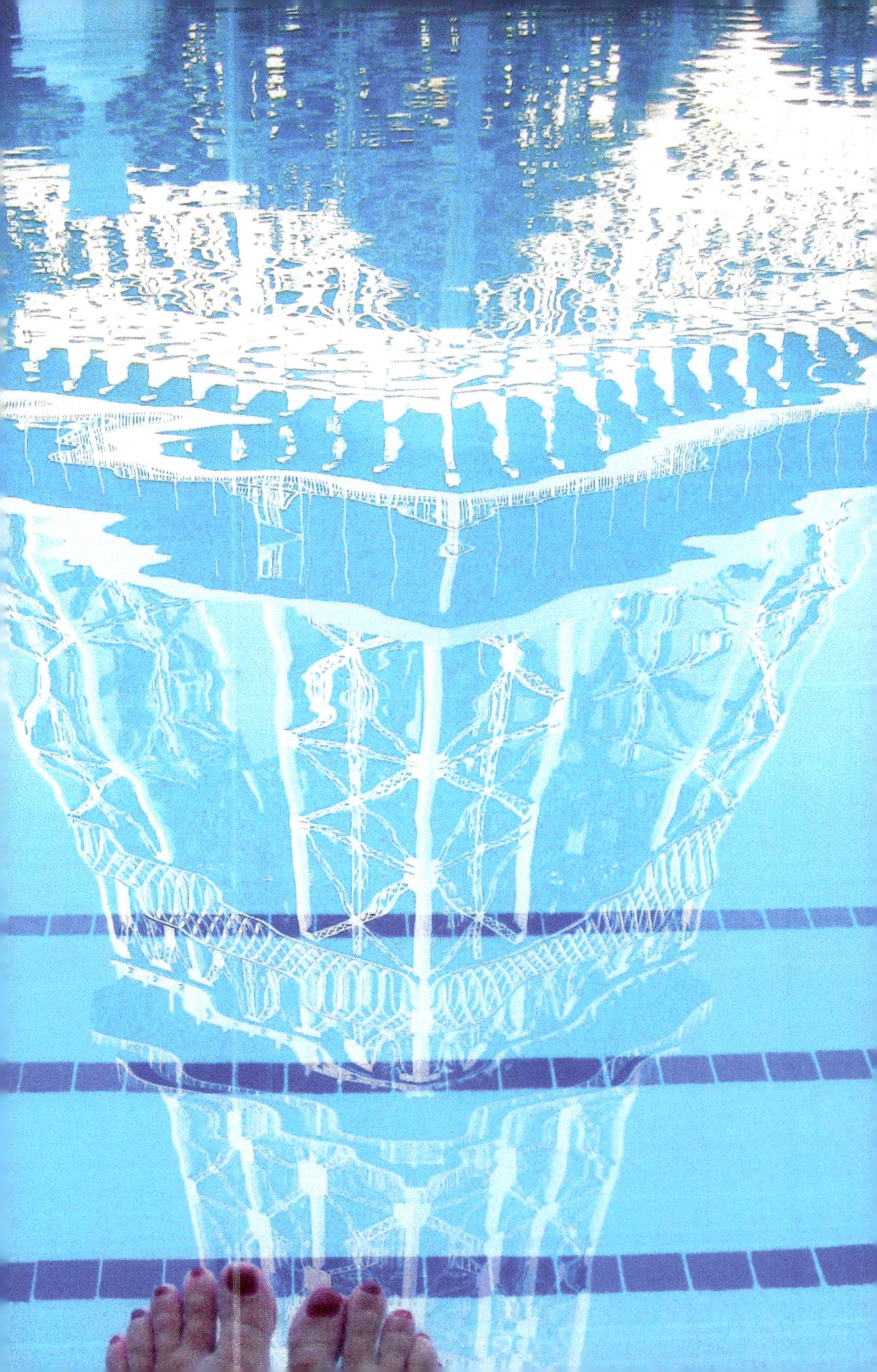

Las Vegas

She is close, as close to *it*
as she is to the pool:
her pretty feet hanging over the chaise lounge—
almost touching
the azure-blue.

Last night, after their barbecue,
after the margaritas
were depleted, guests schmoozed & sent home,

she wasn't surprised
when her husband greeted her
     like a wrecking ball

(she's stopped asking why).
The sun is a ball of fire, falling,
falling.

She adjusts her sunglasses;
can feel the skin around her right eye complicating—
turning the color
of mother of pearl.

She rolls a glass of club soda
across her thigh, over the splay of wine roses
he put there.

She flinches
at the groan of his car in the garage,
then his golf shoes clicking across the clean floor—
"Pamela?!"

The knife that cut the lime for her drink
winks at her
from its station on the patio table.

She has crossed a desert to get to this place—
sore, stiff as a wooden horse.

If he smells like scotch, if he's brought gold tulips,
if the temperature creeps up
a single notch—she *will*,
she swears it.

The Tongue-Tied Moon, 1969

I adored the attention: three fit little men

shimmying across my face,
examining my pores.

I loved their urgent patter—
back & forth, back & forth

then to the rapt masses way down
on Earth:

"A small step & a giant leap . . ."
& the swell of applause

& a billion tiny eyes
on me:

How I longed to make a statement

but the astronauts packed up,
my audience grew distracted

(mortgages, rock & roll, a microscopic war)

before I could open my mouth,
think of the thing to say.

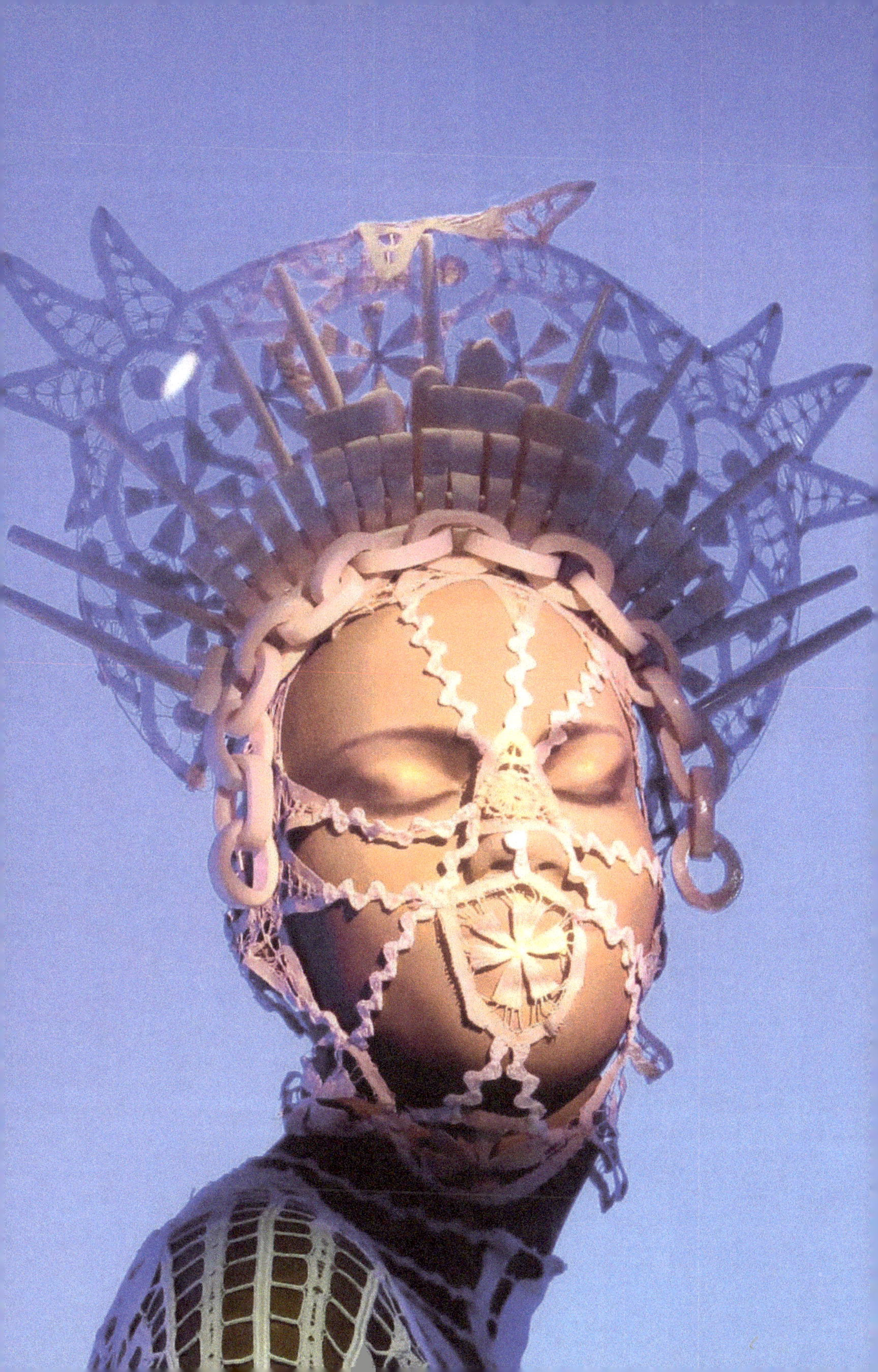

The Defiant Body

Needs to be unique:
left-handed,
      beige & allergic,
ectomorphic—flummoxing me
      & the doctors, whose smug roadmaps
                    get them lost every time
around the slick loop-da-loops
      of those peculiar intestines—

          Who put the kidneys there?

The defiant body—emboldened & shy—
has two left breasts,
one deaf ear
      & a periwinkle eye, lazy as July
            but oddly philosophical.

Right now the thyroid is gently expanding like a helium balloon

& the heart moves
            to its own eccentric beat—
      a spirited but homely dancer.

The menstrual cycle, too, is on a Dali-esque clock,
prompting the nurses in white to throw up their hands,
wonder how the damn thing works.

But perhaps
only because I *can't* shake it off,

I have learned to love
a body
      that lives to break rules.

& it will do what I ask it to—
I think it will do it!—
but when it's good & ready,

      when the body says *now*.

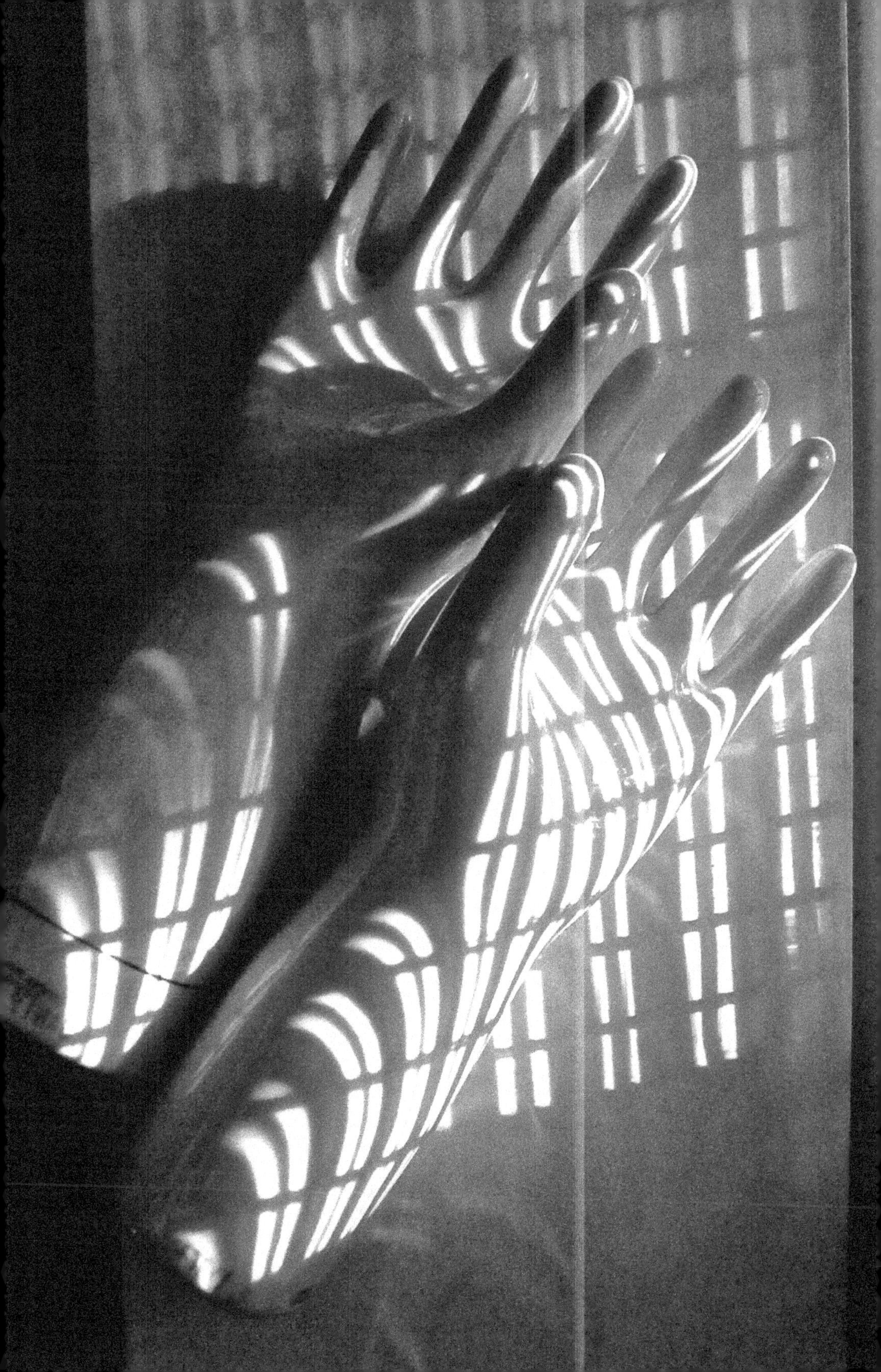

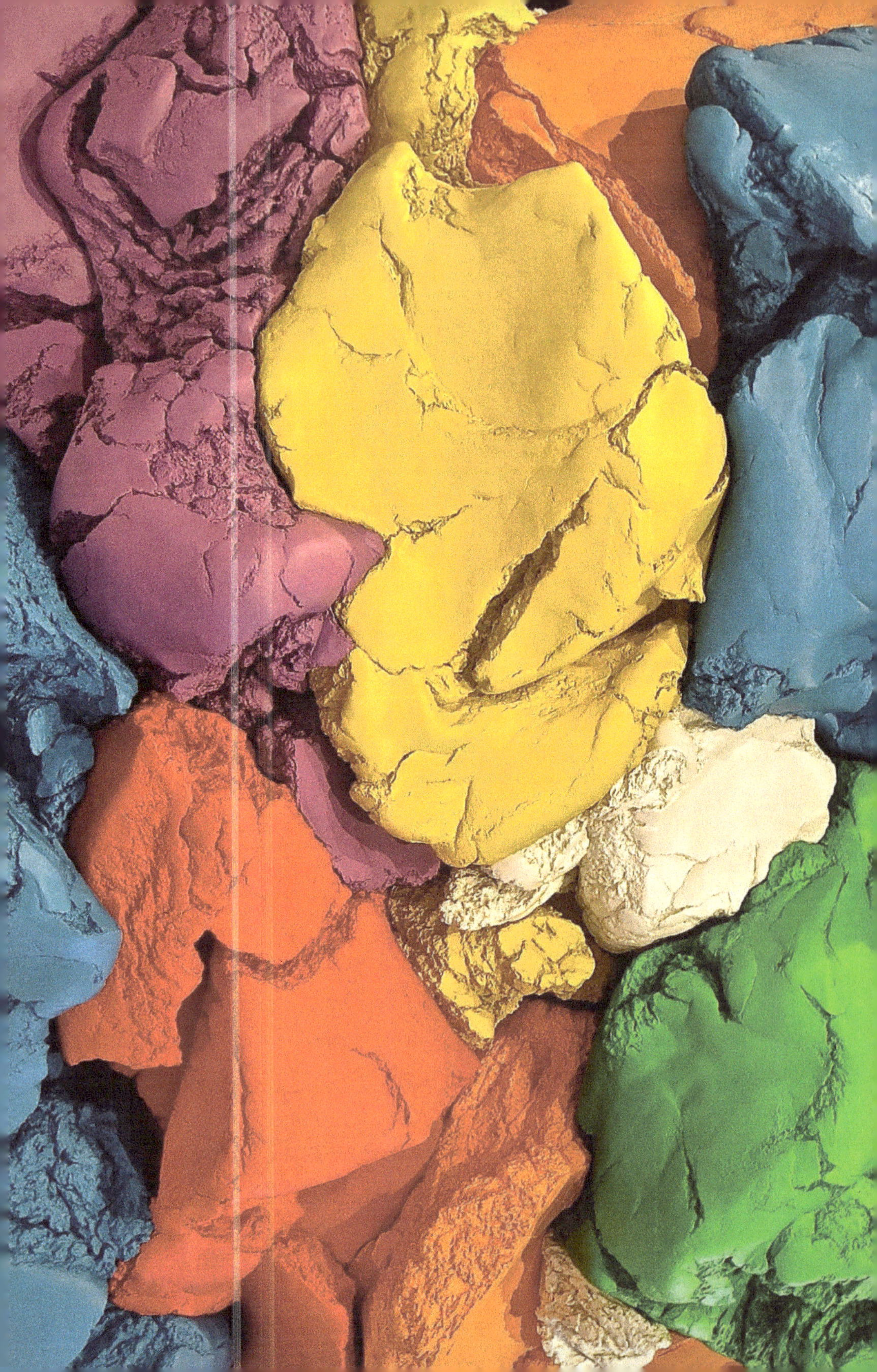

Words for Tyreek

I am helping Tyreek read.
It is a slow, sweaty process
like building a road.

All around,
his classmates sit,
their blue & green storybooks flung open
like butterfly wings—with strings of sentences
just flying out

till one child has to clap her hands over her ears
to soften all the bright singing.

But the words don't speak to Tyreek.
They're mismatched families
of slashes, curls & dots—
floating across the page, mischievously
switching places.

So Tyreek cheats:
each day he memorizes the ornate shapes
of a few new words,
which is hard
because a lot of them look the same—*mean, name, main*—
like the faces of his Aunties.

Today, there are five new words for Tyreek.
He copies them carefully,
unskillfully,
on a sheet of white paper: *cow, bunny, fence, pail* &
tenderly.

"Tenderly!—
Who put that word in there, inside *Peter Rabbit?"*

I tell him what it means.

Then everything is *tenderly*:
the way the sunlight sleeps on that sick, yellow-green plant
on the window sill,
the school clock's *tock*
& the cautious way his teacher, Mrs. Clark, repeats
his five fine words—
as if they're bone china.

After class, Mrs. Clark says she thinks it's nice that
Tyreek got *tenderly*
& has it all to himself.

Next year, Tyreek will repeat the first grade.

I imagine he's home now. His grandmother's asleep &
his much-older brother is speaking
in covert hisses to a girl behind a sealed door. It's cold.
Tyreek sits Indian style in the blue light of the TV:

watching a movie
about a robber in a rich, red car,
occasionally thinking of *tenderly*.

 WHY HAPPINESS MAKES ME NERVOUS

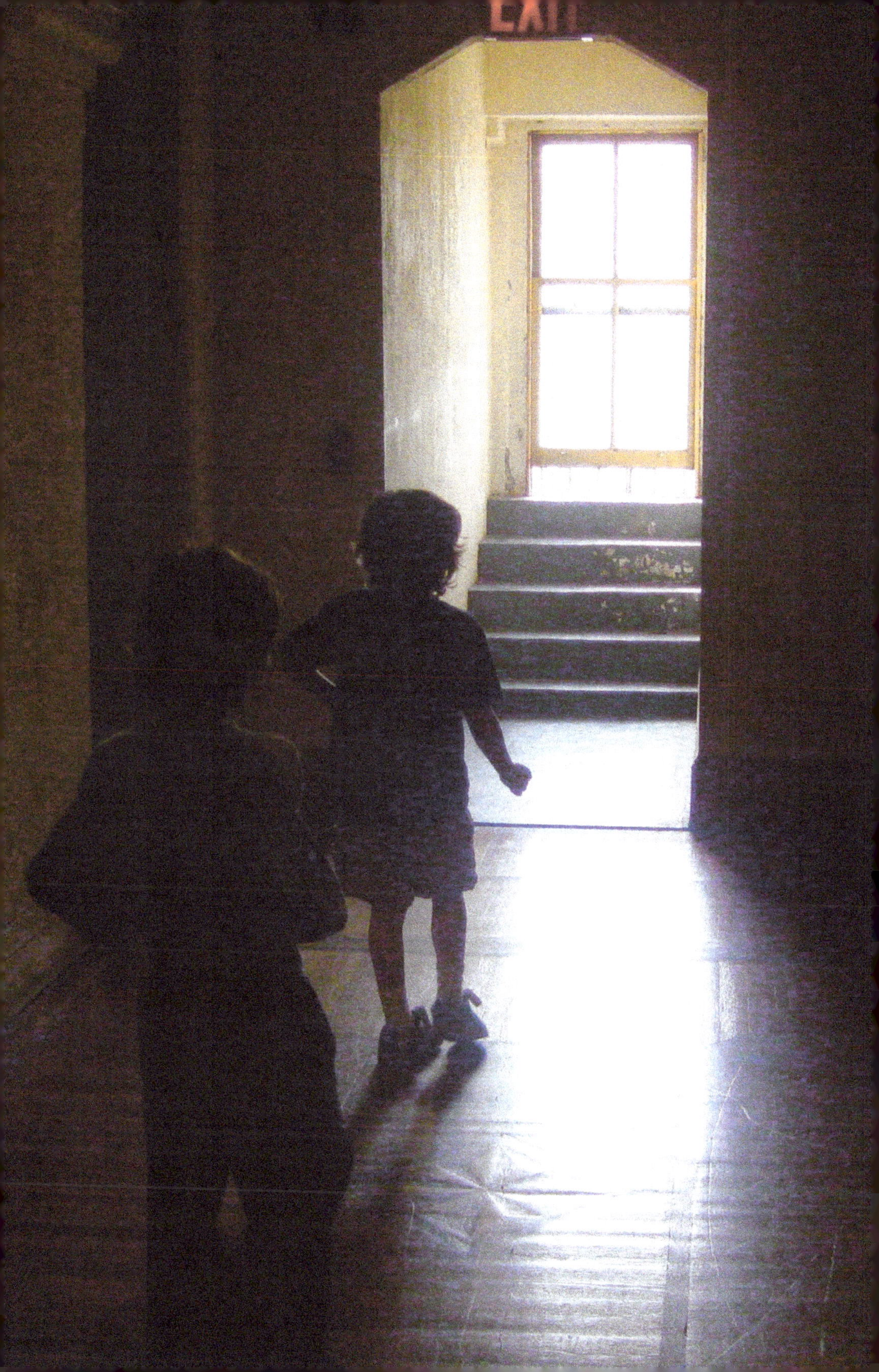
EXIT

Rorschachs of My Father

I see a man with a brush cut on a giraffe
           dispensing jellybeans & bedtime tunes from a polka-dot coat.

I see a thin engineer with a genius IQ
who cannot hold a job,
sit still in a chair—

a father tossing me up up up in the air
                  then walking away to pick up the phone:

It's his secretary. (He loves her!)

I see a guy leaving my mother for dead.

I see the hands
that built a dollhouse equipped with a doorbell & tiny electric lights.

I see an entertainer pulling bright quips from his hat
                    to the delight of the party guests

then
a mean drunk inspiring the same to dump martinis on his head.

           I see a guy who does & doesn't give a fuck—

sailing garish Christmas cards through the mail,
anticipating replies from his four grown kids

                that never come.

I see a husband in a bed with half-moon specs,
           growing increasingly agitated with his sequel wife—

           taking a hammer to their life

because he can,
because *he* should be in Paris!

I see a man superior to everyone & nobody,
loved & unloved &

floating
           like lonely milkweed
                away.

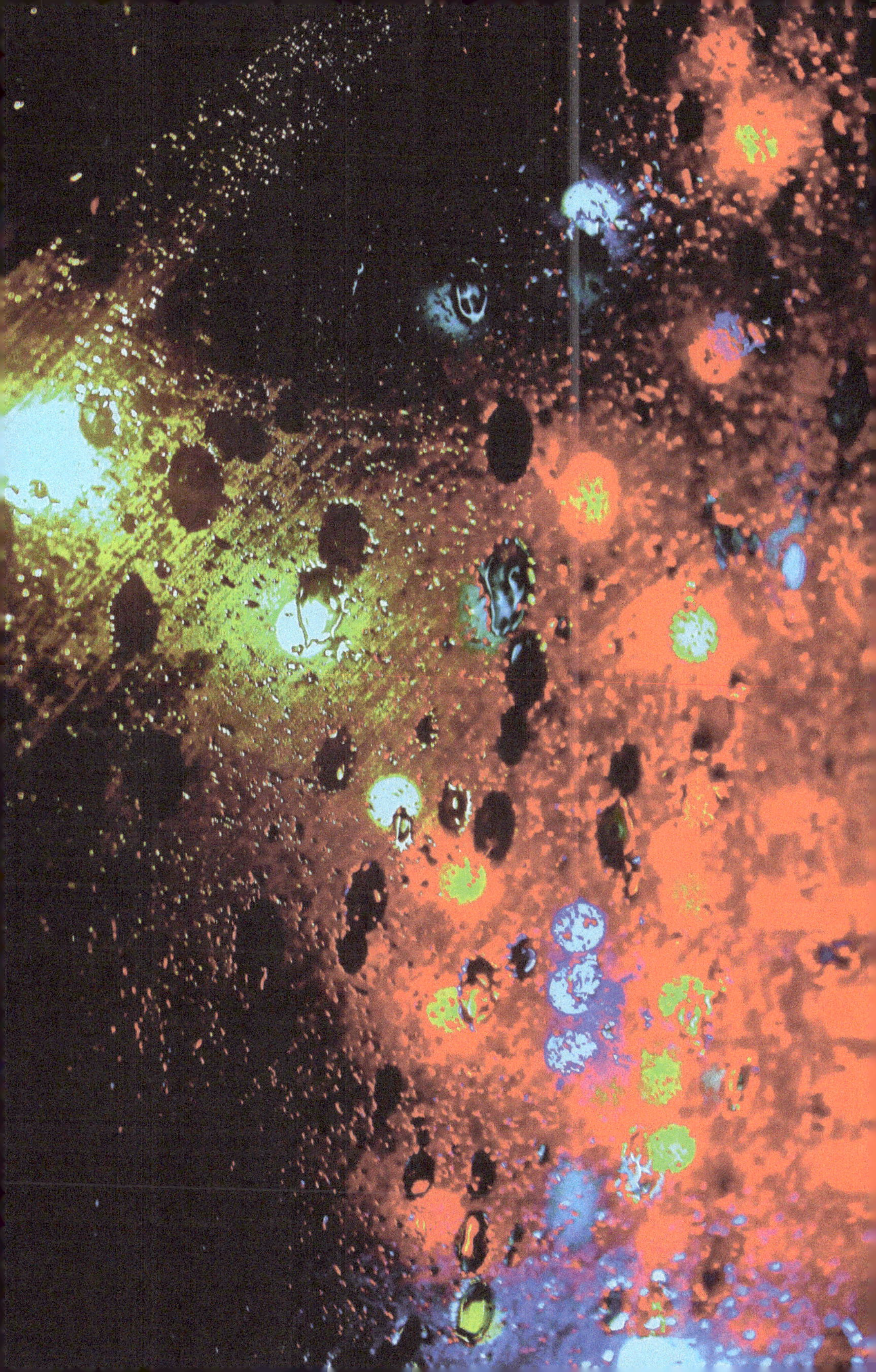

Open Call

The most brilliant one alive—step up!
Man, woman, child!
Tell us, what is your name?
Where do you reside?

A geodesic dome of your own design?

Or a sad box of bricks,
where you process the most startling theories in your head,
the mice stirring,
your synapses aglow—
a private string of Christmas lights.

Are you celebrated?

Or cast out—
your concepts too bright
for anyone else to see.
Are there even words for what you know?
& when you try to explain, does everyone think you're nuts—
their bland eyes shallow
as kiddy pools?

Is your genius-genius benevolent
or a festering grenade?
Tell us,
can you love someone?
Can we love you?

 WHY HAPPINESS MAKES ME NERVOUS

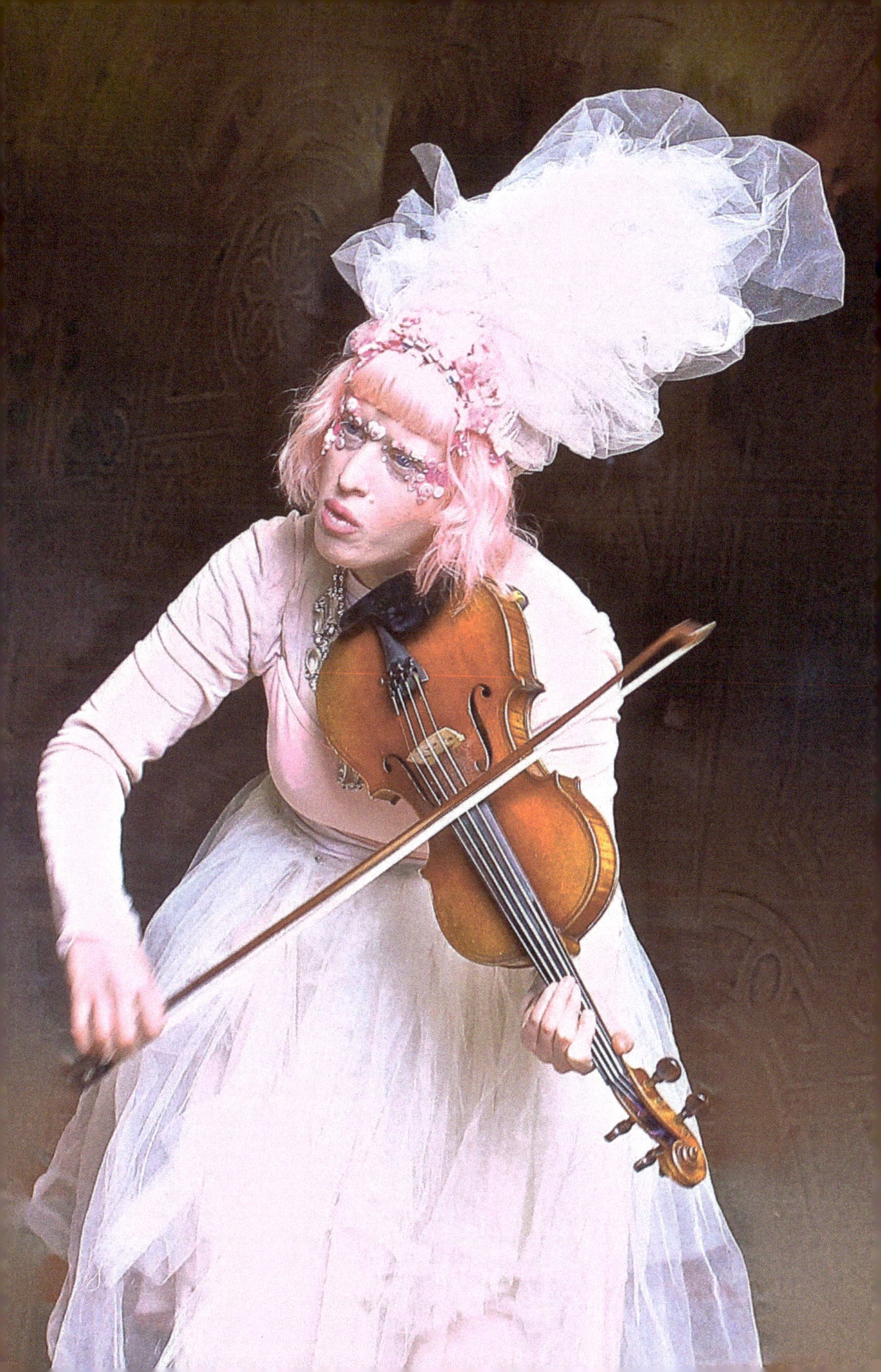

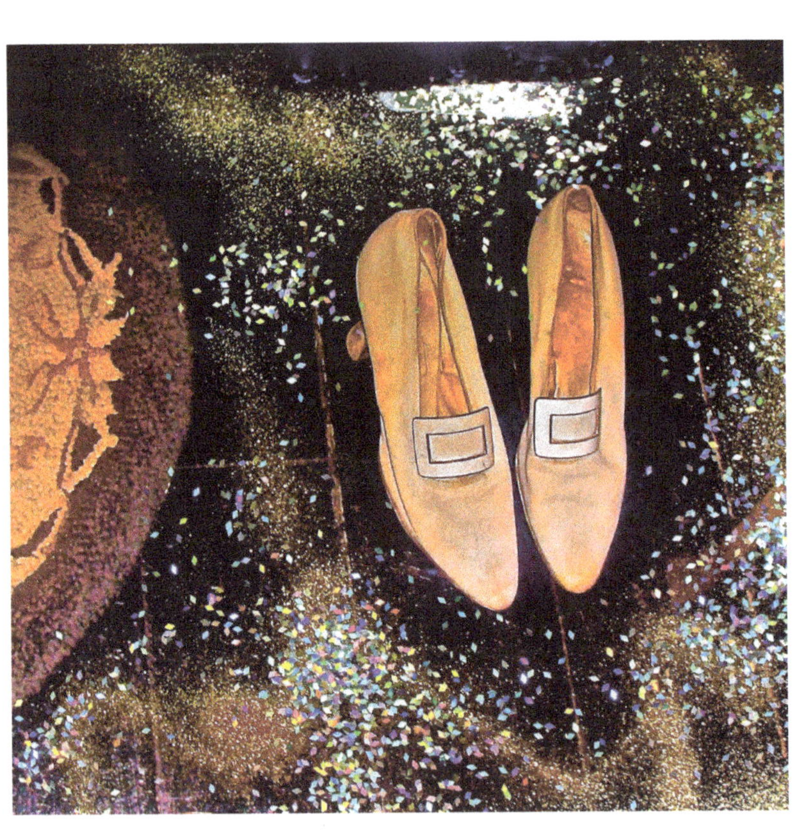

Golden Years

Your arms will hang like empty socks.
Your muscles will rot like an old elastic bra.
Reach the top shelf, middle shelf, bottom shelf? Uh-uh.

Your tin cans will topple. The hair will fall out of your head
& sprout on your knees. A scrim of amber will coat your corneas,
Staining everything you see:

Amber lamp, amber quilt, amber chair.

Arteries will jam like traffic. Bones will parch.
It will take you all day to cross the carpet & turn on the TV,
Only to shout: *Who are these people?*

The pain in your left hip is a red button being pushed
Forever. But you cannot lift your pillbox.
You will outlive your spouse & a horde of cats.

Your sweet tooth will crumble.
You will forget you loved cotton candy.
You will forget you loved.

You will tell time by the church chimes.

                              You will burst into flames
& your children, scattered in their upstate towns,
Won't be able to run down fast enough to put you out.

Aprons

When I was little, my mother wore an apron.
It was blue gingham & had big pockets
trimmed with rickrack.
I liked to say *rickrack*.

I don't recall what she put in those pockets.

When Mom made cookies,
it was ritual for me to lick the beaters.
Eating uncooked batter can cause salmonella,
but the Surgeon General didn't care about that then—
too busy studying the effects of tiny cigarettes on lab mice.

In 1968, my mother quit smoking for good.

Years later, when we were moving,
after my parents had bitterly uncoupled,
I found that apron balled up behind our breadbox.
It was the mid 70s
& women didn't wear them anymore

or cook in high heels.

Hal Gondersson, our next-door neighbor,
sometimes wore an apron though.
It said *BBQ Chefs Make Better Lovers*.
My mother dated him briefly during the Bicentennial
after his wife, Patsy, passed away from Lymphoma.

I miss her pretty hand waving hello across the crocus bed.

Sophomore year, I took the apron with me to college
& wore it to type term papers. It became a gimmick of sorts.
My boyfriend thought I was cute.
Nowadays, men take pride in cooking things
other than scrambled eggs. My brother's specialty is paella.
He used to have a German-Colombian girlfriend with violet eyes,
but she broke his heart like a dry wishbone.

A theory holds that this event inspired his drinking.

My mother still likes to cook.
When she makes an epic meal, i.e. Thanksgiving,
she cranks up the Supremes & puts on a sacrificial T-shirt,
which gets caked with yams & spinach, stewed tomatoes, gravy
& magenta pinpricks of cranberry

that rise from the pot
                    then float down like miniscule paratroopers.

Sometimes
Mom sits down at the table without even changing—
powdered in flour, passing the turkey
to whichever hands flutter
beside her.

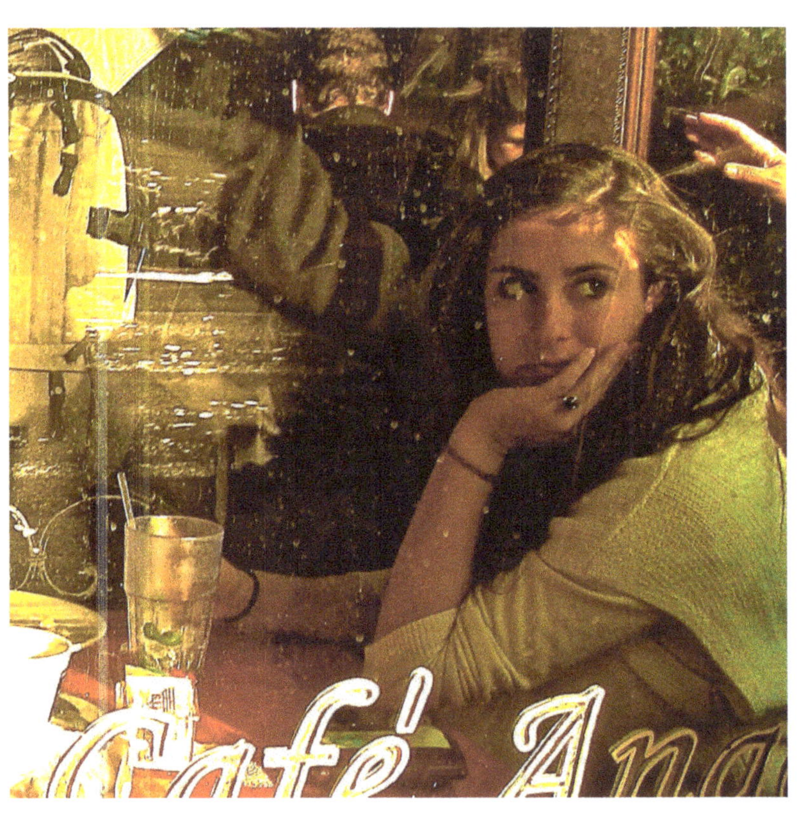

Café Ana

Birthday Drinks With Maria

On the day she turned 36,
Maria's sadness
beat
at exactly the center.

"What's wrong?"
"I'm not sure."

"What's wrong?"
"I'm not sure."

Our sentences coupled,
but didn't speak,
like shy dance partners.

So we smoked on,
depleting ¼ of the Glenlivet birthday bottle:
a clock that says it's time to go.
But instead, Maria opted to cry, confiding,

The sorrow wasn't any one thing:
the defunct fling,
the kidlessness,
or her parents—they had always loved her
appropriately—
nothing like that!

"It's just . . ."

Then Maria began to speak,
molding her tangled, wet words
into an insight
that went something like this:

she had always expected life's center
to be the best, the tenderest part

like an artichoke's heart

& having just arrived,
she was sorry to learn that hers
was not.

Happily Ever After
—for Sleeping Beauty

She was beautiful
even when spinning wool,
even the day she encountered the thorn:
blood blooming red
on her index finger, then eyelids closing down.

Witnesses report a long, lush sigh rushed from her lips
like a satin ribbon
as she exquisitely
slipped
to the palace floor.

On a jewel-encrusted bed,
she slept for 100 years: beyond images & anything untoward—
her even breath, a cocktail of roses;
her yellow hair splayed on the pillow
like the sun on a fine day.

& when *he* kissed her,
she opened her turquoise eyes on a new world
& it was ecstasy:
Not waves of joy,
with rising & falling points of glory,

but the crest-of-the-crest of the wave *forever*.

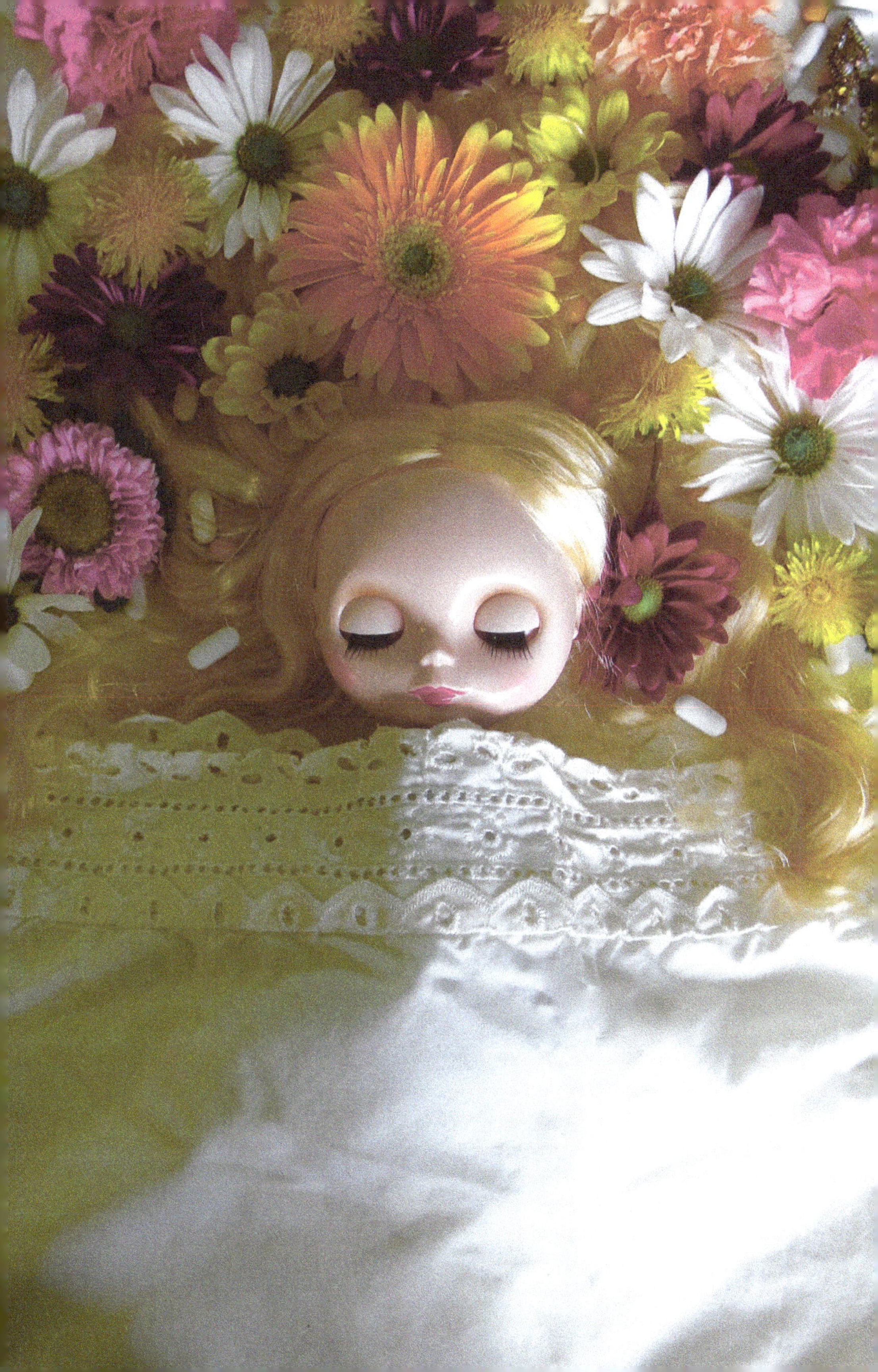

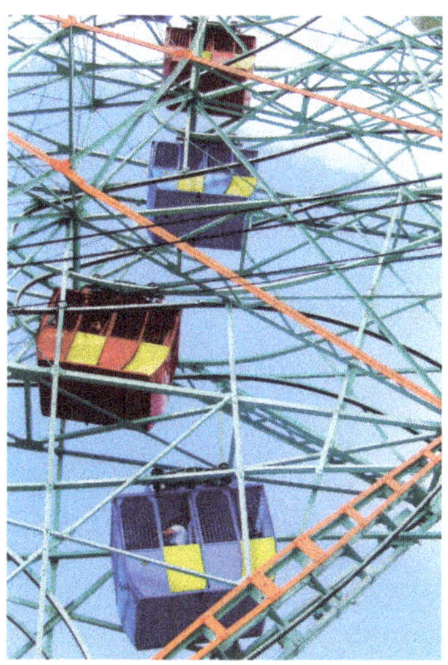

Acknowledgments

Enormous thanks to the many people who made this book possible, chief among them Deborah Emin of Sullivan Street Press, who invited me to "put on a show" with poems and pictures. I am so grateful for your enthusiasm, wisdom, and unflagging belief in my ability. Thanks as well to Deborah's kind and resourceful partner, Suzanne Pyrch. Heartfelt appreciation to Maria Lilja for her exquisite cover concept and the talented Bethany Luckenbach of Scribe for her seamless interior design. Praise to the poets who inspired me and the teachers who helped me hone my craft—especially the marvelous Martha Rhodes. Gratitude to the gifted William Eggleston, whose Whitney photo exhibit moved me to pick up a camera and get out in the real world. Thanks to the Charlesworth clan for their continued support, including my amazing writer of a mom, Sylvia, and her caring partner, Gerald Kressman, as well as my incredible siblings, Jacqueline, Greg, and Eric. Thanks to my in-laws, Donna and Rex Martin, who set an example of diligence and craft. Last but not least, a giant, Technicolor shout-out to my rock of a husband, Justin, who cheerfully helped guide my manuscript through its many drafts, and my remarkable twin sons, Dash and Theo—you are my heart.

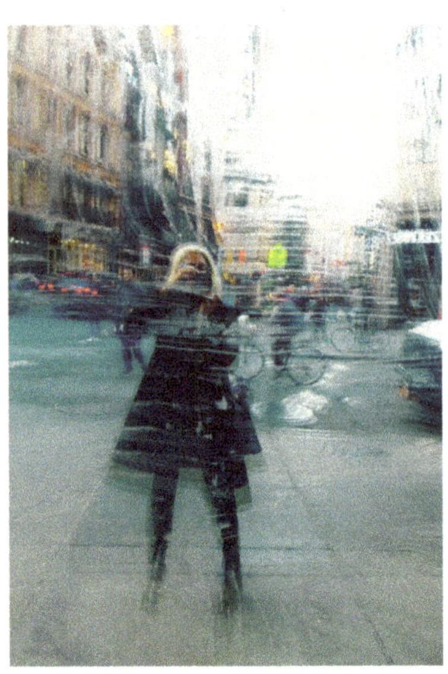

About the Author

Liza Charlesworth is a poet, street photographer, and writer of books for both children and adults, including *Spiderella* (Scholastic Inc.) and *The Couple's Guide to In Vitro Fertilization* (Da Capo Press). Liza's poems have appeared in numerous publications, and her photos can be viewed at her tumblr site, Beautyhog (lizacharlesworth1.tumblr.com). She lives in New York City with her husband and twin sons, who provide daily inspiration.